W. H. (William Henry) Withrow

The native races of North America

W. H. (William Henry) Withrow

The native races of North America

ISBN/EAN: 9783742863409

Manufactured in Europe, USA, Canada, Australia, Japa

Cover: Foto ©Suzi / pixelio.de

Manufactured and distributed by brebook publishing software
(www.brebook.com)

W. H. (William Henry) Withrow

The native races of North America

THE

NATIVE RACES

OF

NORTH AMERICA.

. . .

EDITED BY

W. H. WITHROW, D.D., F.R.S.C.

. . .

TORONTO:

WILLIAM BRIGGS,

WESLEY BUILDINGS.

MONTREAL: C. W. COATES.   HALIFAX: S. F. HUESTIS.
1895.

CONTENTS.

[NOTE.—The Editor lays little claim to originality in the compilation of this book. He has been largely dependent upon the writings of others for the information it contains. For a number of the excellent cuts which are printed in this volume he is indebted to the courtesy of the Rev. E. R. Young, and also for the kind permission to reprint sections of his interesting volumes, "By Canoe and Dog Train" and "Indian Wigwams and Northern Camp Fires." He begs also to acknowledge indebtedness to the admirable volume of the Rev. John McLean, Ph.D., on "The Indians of Canada," and for the extracts acknowledged elsewhere from the Rev. J. Semmens, the Rev. J. McDougall and other writers who have admirably treated this theme. —W. H. W.]

CONTENTS.

	PAGE
WAMPUM	91
MISSION WORK	92
POTLACH	100
REV. GEORGE McDOUGALL	101
SUN DANCE	107
INDIAN POVERTY	110
INDIAN SCHOOLS	113
HOW INDIANS TREAT THE AGED	117
CHRISTIANITY AND THE SIOUX	121
NORTH-WEST MISSIONS	123
THE SONG OF HIAWATHA	140
PICTURE WRITING	141
WINTER AND FAMINE	143
DEATH OF MINNEHAHA	144
THE PROPHECY	146
THE MISSIONARY	147
MISSIONS IN LABRADOR	149
MISSION BOAT "EVANGELIST"	152
MISSION LIFE IN THE FAR NORTH	154
THE HUDSON'S BAY COMPANY	156
PAKAN, THE INDIAN CHIEF	162
INDIAN MISSIONS IN BRITISH COLUMBIA	168
FORT SIMPSON MISSION	176
SABBATH-KEEPING INDIANS	180
NAAS RIVER MISSION	183
REV THOMAS CROSBY	191
THE "GLAD TIDINGS"	199

THE NATIVE RACES OF NORTH AMERICA.

THE name Indians, given to the native races of America, commemorates the mistaken idea of its discoverers, that they had reached the shores of the Asiatic continent. A short account of these races, and of their character, custom, and tribal divisions, is necessary in order to understand the long and cruel conflict between the white man and the red for the possession of the New World.

All over the North American continent, from Lake Superior to the Gulf of Mexico, from the Alleghanies to the Rocky Mountains, are found the remains of an extinct and pre-historic people. These remains consist, for the most part, of earthen mounds, often of vast extent and almost countless numbers. Hence their unknown creators are called the Mound-Builders. These strange structures may be divided into two classes : Enclosures and Mounds proper. The chief purpose of the Enclosures seems to have been for defence—the formation, as it were, of a fortified camp. They were sometimes of great size, covering many hundreds of acres. They were surrounded by parapets of earth, in the form of circles, octagons, or similar figures. They were evidently designed for protection against an intrusive race, and formed a line of forts from the Alleghanies to the Ohio. Another striking form of enclosure is that designated

ANIMAL MOUNDS IN WISCONSIN.

1, Turtle mound, 306 feet long, 6 feet high; 7 and 8, lizard mounds, 8 with curved tail; 9, cruciform figure, 209 feet long, 72 feet wide; 3 and 4, fox figures; 5, bear; 14, buffalo; 12, 13, 10, and 6, bird-like forms.

Animal Mounds. These are outlines in earth-work, in low relief, of sacred animals—probably the totems of different tribes, as the turtle, lizard, serpent, alligator, eagle, buffalo, and the like. They are especially numerous in the Valley of the Wisconsin. The " Great Serpent " of Adams County, Ohio, is over a thousand feet long, and the " Alligator " of Licking

County is two hundred and fifty feet long and fifty feet broad.

The mounds proper are of much less extent, but of greater elevation. Some, there is reason to believe, from the presence of charred bones, charcoal, trinkets, etc., were used as altars for the burning of sacrifice,

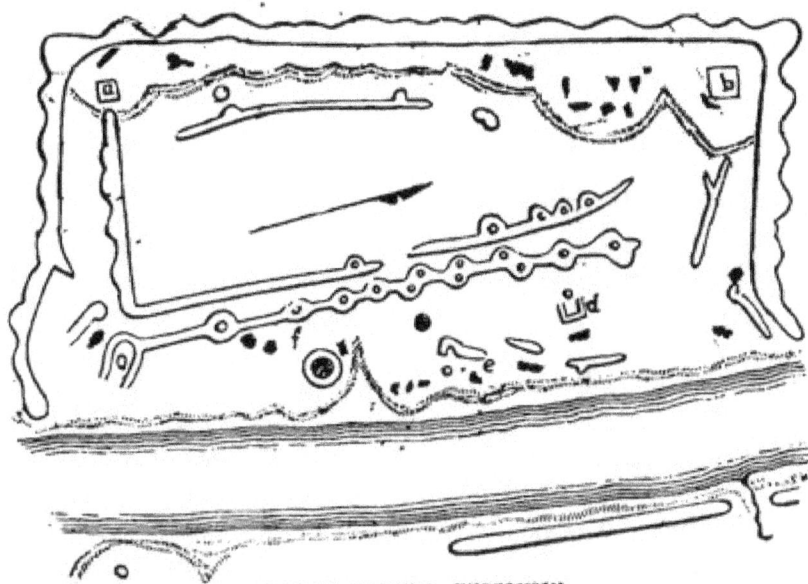

ANCIENT MOUNDS, WISCONSIN.

Length, 1,419 feet; width, 7,000 feet; a, b, c, and d, pyramid-shaped figures; e and f, deep depressions.

and perhaps for the offering of human victims. Others are know as Temple Mounds. These were chiefly truncated pyramids, with graded approaches to their tops, which are always level, and are sometimes fifty feet in height. In Mexico and Central

America this class is represented by vast structures, faced with flights of steps and surmounted by temples of stone.

More numerous than any are the Sepulchral Mounds. They always contain the remains of one or more bodies, accompanied by trinkets, cups, and vases, probably once containing food provided by living hands for the departed spirit faring forth, as was fondly believed, on its unknown journey to the happy hunting-grounds beyond the sky. The size of these is generally inconsiderable; but they sometimes attain great magnitude, in which case they probably cover the remains of some distinguished chief. One of these, known as Grave Creek Mound, in Virginia, is seventy feet in height and nine hundred feet in circumference. Sometimes earthen vessels are found, containing charred human remains, indicating the practice of cremation among the Mound-Builders.

But there are other evidences of the comparatively high state of civilization of those remarkable people. There are numerous remains of their art and manufactures. Among these are flint arrow-heads and axes, pestles and mortars for grinding corn, and pipes, frequently elaborately carved with considerable artistic skill. These last often occur in the form of animal or human figures, sometimes exhibiting much grotesque humor, and frequently executed in very intractable material. Remains of closely woven textile fabrics have also been found, together with implements used in the spinning of the thread and manufacture of the cloth. The pottery and other wares of the Mound-

Builders exhibit graceful forms, elegant ornamenta-
tion, and much skill in manufacture. On some of

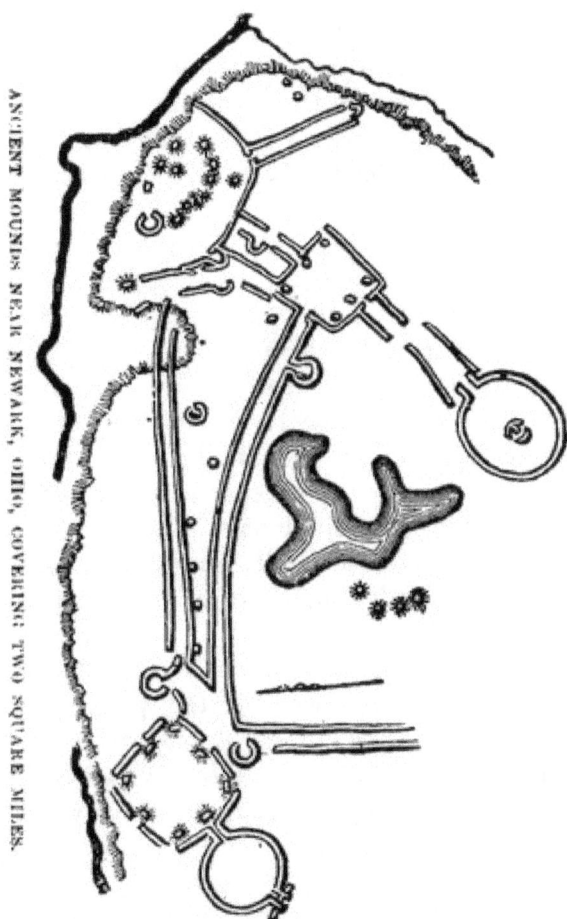

ANCIENT MOUNDS NEAR NEWARK, OHIO, COVERING TWO SQUARE MILES.

these the human face and form are delineated with
much fidelity and grace, and the features differ widely

from those of the present race of Indians. Copper implements, the work of this strange people, are also found in considerable quantities. Among these are knives, chisels, axes, spear and arrow-heads, bracelets, and personal ornaments. Many of these implements exhibit on their surface the unmistakable traces of the moulds in which they were cast, showing that their manufacturers understood the art of reducing or at least of fusing metals.

But the most striking proof of the mechanical skill of the Mound-Builders is their extensive mining operations on the south shore of Lake Superior. Here are a series of mines and drifts, sometimes fifty feet deep, extending for many miles along the shore ; at Ontonagon and at Isle Royal, off the north shore. In one of these was found, at the depth of eighteen feet, resting on oaken sleepers, a mass of native copper weighing over six tons, which had been raised five feet from its original bed; numerous props, levers, ladders, and shovels, employed in mining operations, were also found.

These old miners had become extinct long before the discovery of America, for the present race of Indians had no knowledge of copper when first visited by white men; and trees, whose concentric rings indicated an age of four hundred years, have been found growing upon the accumulated rubbish that filled the shafts.

The commerce of the Mound-Builders was also quite extensive. Copper from these northern mines is found widely distributed through eighteen degrees of latitude, from Lake Superior to the Gulf of Mexico. Iron was also brought from Missouri, mica from North Carolina, and obsidian from Mexico.

An examination of the skulls of those pre-historic people, scattered over a wide area, indicates, together with other evidences, that they were a mild, unwarlike race, contented to toil like the Egyptian serfs in the vast and profitless labours of mound-building. Agriculture must have received among them a high degree of development, in order to the maintenance of the populous communities by which the huge mounds were constructed. Their principal food was probably maize, the most prolific cereal in the world.

The question, "Who were the Mound-Builders?" only involves the inquirer in the mazes of conjecture. They seem to have been of the same race with the ancient people of Mexico, Central America and Peru. They probably came, by way of Behring's Strait, from the great central Asiatic plateau, which has been, through the ages, the fruitful birth-place of nations. As they advanced towards the tropical and equatorial regions of the continent, they seem to have developed the civilization which met the astonished eyes of Cortes and Pizarro. Successive waves of Asiatic emigration of a fierce and barbarous race, apparently expelled them from the Mississippi Valley and drove them south of the Rio Grande. Probably little will ever be known of their history unless some new Champollion shall arise to decipher the strange hieroglyphics which cover the rocky tablets of the ruined cities of Yucatan and Guatemala.

The Cliff-Dwellers.

Akin to the Mound Builders were the Cliff-Dwellers. Of this strange people and their struc-

CLIFF-DWELLINGS.

tures we will give, with appropriate illustrations, a brief account.

One of the most interesting exhibits at the Chicago Fair was that of the Cliff-Dwellers. A large covered mound represented one of the Black Hills of the far West. In the interior of this were reproductions on a reduced scale, as well as one or two in large size, of the strange cliff-dwellings. An admirable museum of the remains of the Cliff-Dwellers, their pottery, utensils, weapons, tools, their spinning, weaving, and the like, and their mummies and skeletons, in a measure enabled us to reproduce the old life of the Cliff-Dwellers.

In the south-western portion of the United States Territories, beyond the Rio Grande River, is a vast plateau stretching to the base of the Sierra Nevadas. Various large streams have cut long canyons through the nearly horizontal strata, in places to a depth of six or seven thousand feet. In the greater part of this region there is little moisture apart from those streams, and, as a consequence, vegetation is very sparse, and the general aspect of the country is that of a semi-desert. Yet there is abundant evidence that at one time it supported a numerous population. "There is scarcely a square mile of the six thousand examined," writes Professor W. H. Holmes, "that does not furnish evidence of previous occupation by a race totally distinct from the nomadic savages who now hold it, and in many ways superior to them."

The ruins are almost exclusively stone structures. Brick or wood seldom occurs. They may be classed, as to situation, as follows : (1) Lowland or agricultural dwellings ; (2) cave-dwellings ; and (3) cliff-houses or fortresses.

Those of the first class are chiefly on the river-bottoms, or the fertile lands near the water, without reference to defence. The second class are excava-

CAVE-DWELLINGS.

tions in the faces of the low bluffs, and are chosen chiefly for concealment and security. Those of the third class are built high up in steep and inaccessible cliffs, and are evidently places of refuge and strongholds for defence. During seasons of war and invasion, families were probably sent to them for security, while the warriors went forth to battle; "and one can readily imagine," says Professor Holmes, "that when the hour of total defeat had come they served as a last resort for a disheartened and desperate people."

In some cases the ruins give evidence of the well-built and solid walls of a fortress, which must have possessed considerable strength.

The cave-dwellings are made by digging irregular cavities in the faces of bluffs and cliffs of friable rock, and then walling up the fronts, leaving only small doorways and an occasional small window.

The cliff-houses are of firm, neat masonry, and the manner in which they are attached or connected to the cliffs is simply marvellous. They conform in shape to the floor or roof of the niche or shelf on which they are built, which has been worn away by the natural erosion of the elements. Their construction has cost a great deal of labour, the stones and mortar having been brought for hundreds of feet up the most precipitous places. In many places the larger mortar seams have been chinked with bits of pottery and sandstone. The marks of the mason's pick are as fresh as if made within a few years, and the fine, hard mud mortar, which has been applied with the bare hands, still retain impressions of the minute markings of the skin of the fingers.

In some cases the houses are cleverly hidden away

CLIFF-DWELLINGS.

in the dark recesses, and so very like the surrounding cliffs in colour, that I had almost completed the sketch of the upper house before the lower one was detected. They are at least eight hundred feet above the river. The lower four hundred feet is of rough broken slope, the remainder of massive bedded sandstone, full of wind-worn niches, crevices and caves.

On the face of the smooth and almost perpendicular cliff a sort of stairway, of small niches in the rock, has been cut. An enemy would have but small chance of reaching and entering such a fortress if defended even by women and children. There is evidence that a trickling stream of water supplied the inhabitants with this vital necessity.

A large cave town occurs in a great ledge or bench of an encircling line of cliffs. The total length of the solidly built portion is eight hundred and forty-five feet, with a width of about forty-five feet. It contains about seventy-five distinct rooms, probably distinct dwellings.

On the Colorado Chiquito occurs the somewhat formidable-looking fortress shown on page 18. So difficult of access is this that our author thinks it must have been reached by a rope-ladder. A similar cliff-dwelling is shown in the cut on page 14, commanding a broad outlook over valley and river far below.

Among the *debris* of the cliff-houses are large quantities of pottery—some of very elegant shape, and ornamented with very handsome designs ; some will hold as much as ten gallons. The makers evidently

2

had a considerable imitative ability and sense of grotesque humor, as many of their wares were capital representations of fowls and the like, often with a very comic look. Specimens of woven fabric and little images, probably for idolatrous use, occur. Hieroglyphic or picture-writing is also found engraved in the rock, or painted with red and white pigments. A number of well-shaped skulls have also been found.

Who were the Cliff-Dwellers and what was their fate? is a question of great interest. In the plains of Arizona and New Mexico are numerous Pueblo villages, numbering about seven thousand inhabitants, who are considered to be the descendants of the Cliff-Dwellers. They dwell in large communities—from three hundred to seven hundred souls—in one huge structure. This structure consists of a hollow square, surrounded on three sides with buildings of *adobe*, or mud brick, in two or three receding stories. These Pueblo Indians exhibit about the same grade of civilization as the Cliff-Dwellers, and it is conjectured that the latter retired southward some time since the Spanish occupation of Central America, either on account of the hostile pressure of fiercer tribes from the north, or from the failure of the means of sustenance through the drying up of the streams.

Sir Daniel Wilson expresses the opinion, founded largely on the evidence of language and architectural remains, that the earliest current of New World population "spread through the islands of the Pacific and reached the South American continent long before an excess of Asiatic population had diffused itself into

its own inhospitable steppes."—" Pre-historic Man,"
pp. 604-605. He also thinks that another wave of
population reached Central America and Brazil by the
Canaries and Antilles, and that then the intrusive
race, from which our Indians have sprung, arrived by
way of Behring's Strait, driving the Mound-Builders
before them.

Indian Characteristics.

This intruding race was of a fierce and warlike
character, and, continuing its nomad life, never
attained to a degree of civilization at all comparable
to that of the race which they dispossessed. They
have certain common characteristics, though with
numerous minor tribal distinctions of aspect, language,
and customs. They were, for the most part, a tall,
athletic people, with sinewy forms, regular features,
prominent cheek-bones, straight black hair, sometimes
shaven, scanty beard, dark eyes, which, except when
the passions are roused, are rather sluggish in expression, and copper-coloured skin. In some tribes, as the
Flatheads, the artificial moulding of the skull, by
means of pressure applied in infancy, was common.
They were capable of much endurance of cold,
hunger and fatigue; were haughty, taciturn, and
stoical in their manners; were active, cunning, and
stealthy in war; but in camp were sluggish and
addicted to gluttonous feasts. The women, in youth,
were of agreeable form and feature, but through
severe drudgery soon become withered and course.
The high degree of health and vigor of the race was

INDIANS AT HOME—SKIN TENTS.

probably due to the large mortality of weak or sickly children through the hardships of savage life.

The agriculture of the native tribes, with slight exception, was of the scantiest character—a little patch of Indian corn or tobacco rudely cultivated near their summer cabins. Their chief subsistence was derived from hunting and fishing, in which they became very expert. With flint-headed arrows and spears, and stone axes and knives, they would attack and kill the deer, elk, or buffalo. The necessity of following these objects of their pursuit to their often distant feeding-grounds, precluded social or political organization except within very narrow limits. The same cause also prevented the construction, with a few exceptions, of any but the rudest and simplest dwellings—conical wigwams of skins or birch-bark, spread over a framework of poles. Some of the more settled and agricultural communities had, however, large lodges for public assemblies or feasts, and even for the joint accommodation of several families. Groups of these lodges were sometimes surrounded by palisades, and even by strong defensive works, with heaps of stones to repel attack, and reservoirs of water to extinguish fires kindled by the enemy.

The different tribes of Indians have, most of them, different ways of building their homes, and they are divided and named according to these different methods.

Some, who cover the framework of their wigwams with skins, are called "Skin-Builders;" others form the long prairie grass into graceful structures, and are

called " Grass-Builders ;" still others make a foundation of rough timbers, covering it with a paste made
of tough clay and gravel; these are called " Dirt-
Builders." Others, using wood and timbers in rough
ways, are called " Wood " and " Timber-Builders,"
while the " Bark-Builders " are still another class,
who use the tough and beautiful bark of the birch
tree and fashion it into curious and useful homes.

The Sioux are "Skin-Builders," but the Chippewas
work with birch bark, both in their homes and their
canoes, in a beautiful and artistic way. The Sioux,
the " Skin-Builders," take fifteen or twenty long pine
poles and make a frame work, circular at the bottom
and coming to a point at the top. Over these they
stretch very tight one entire piece of material, formed
from the skins of fifteen or twenty buffaloes or cattle
sewed together. On these skins they paint and
embroider, in most glowing and beautiful colours, large
pictures of horses, men, battle scenes, or anything
which may please their fancy. It may easily be
imagined that these present a beautiful and strange
appearance in a village containing four or five
hundred wigwams. It may be a fact new and
interesting to some of my readers that the word
wigwam is derived from an Indian word, meaning
" home " or " dwelling-place."

The entrances to these homes are very low, but
they grow high and roomy toward the centre, where
there is a small opening to allow smoke to escape.
We would do well to take lessons in dressing skins
from our Indian neighbours, for they prepare them

so carefully that they do not become hard or stiff, but remain soft and pliable, even after they have been thoroughly wet and dried again.

The Chippewa homes, built with the bark, are made upon a light frame of poles, stuck in the ground and bent over a rounding frame at the top, so as to form a roof. These frames are covered with large pieces of the bark, laid on so as to over-lap one another ; and when the tribes move, the bark coverings are taken off, rolled up, and easily carried from place to place.

The triumph of Indian skill and ingenuity was the bark-canoe—a marvel of beauty, lightness and strength. It was constructed of birch-bark, severed in large sheets from the trees, stretched over a slender framework of ribs bent into the desired form, and well gummed at the seams with pine resin. Kneeling in these fragile barks, and wielding a short, strong paddle, the Indian or his squaw would navigate for hundreds of miles the inland waters, shooting the arrowy rapids, and boldly launching upon the stormy lake. Where rocks or cataracts interrupted the progress, the light canoe could easily be carried over the " portage " to the navigable waters beyond.

The Indian dress consisted of skins of wild animals, often ornamented with shells, porcupine quills, and brilliant pigments. In summer, little clothing was worn, but the body was tattooed and painted, or smeared with oil. When on a war expedition the face and figure were bedaubed with startling contrasts of color, as black, white, red, yellow and blue. The

hair was often elaborately decorated with dyed
plumes or crests of feathers. Sometimes the head
was shaved, all but the scalp-lock on the crown. The

INDIAN TYPE—BEARS' CLAWS NECKLACE.

women seldom dressed their hair, and, except in youth,
wore little adornment. Their life after marriage was
one of perpetual drudgery. They tilled the fields,

gathered fuel, bore the burdens on the march, and performed all the domestic duties in camp.

The Indian wars were frequent and fierce, generally springing out of hereditary blood-feuds between tribes, or from the purpose to avenge real or fancied insults or wrongs. After a war-feast and war-dance, in which the plumed and painted " braves " wrought themselves into a frenzy of excitement, they set out on the war-path against the object of their resentment. Stealthily gliding through the forest, they would lie in wait, sometimes for days, for an opportunity of surprising the enemy. With a wild whoop they would burst upon a sleeping village and involve in indiscriminate massacre every age and either sex. Firing the inflammable huts and dragging off their prisoners, they would make a hasty retreat with their victims. Some of these were frequently adopted by the tribe in place of its fallen warriors; others were reserved for fiendish tortures by fire or knife. One trophy they never neglected, if possible, to secure—the reeking scalp-lock of their enemy. Torn with dreadful dexterity from the skull, and dried in the smoke of the hut, it was worn as the hideous proof of the prowess of the savage warrior. When captured, they exhibited the utmost stoicism in the endurance of pain. Amid agonies of torture they calmly sang their death-song, hurling defiance at the foe.

Their councils for deliberation were conducted with great gravity and decorum. The speakers often exhibited much eloquence, wit, vigour of thought, and lively imagination. Their oratory abounded in bold and striking metaphors, and was characterized by great practical shrewdness. They were without a written language, but their treaties were ratified by the exchange of wampum-belts of variegated beads, having definite significations. These served also as memorials of the transaction, and were cherished as the historic records of the tribe.

The Indians were deeply superstitious. Some tribes had an idea of a Great Spirit or Manitou, whose dwelling-place was the sky, where he had provided happy hunting-grounds for his red children after death. Hence they were often buried with their weapons, pipes, ornaments, and a supply of food for their subsistence on their journey to the spirit-world. Others observed a sort of fetichism—the worship of stones, plants, waterfalls, and the like ; and in the thunder, lightning, and tempest they recognized the influence of good or evil spirits. The " medicine-man " or conjuror, cajoled or terrified them by their superstitious hopes or fears. They attached great importance to dreams and omens, and observed rigorous fasts, when they starved themselves to emaciation; and glutton feasts, when they gorged themselves to repletion. They were inveterate and infatuated gamblers, and have been known to stake their lives upon a cast of the dice, and then bend their heads for the stroke of the victor's tomahawk.

In the unhappy conflicts between the English and the French for the possession of the continent, the Indians were the coveted allies of the respective combatants. They were supplied with knives, guns, and ammunition, and the atrocities of savage were added to those of civilized warfare. The profitable trade in peltries early became an object of ambition to the rival nations, and immense private fortunes and public revenue were derived from this source. The white man's "fire-water" and the fatal small-pox wasted the native tribes. The progress of settlement drove them from their ancient hunting-grounds. A chronic warfare between civilization and barbarism raged along the frontier, and dreadful scenes of massacre and reprisal stained with blood the annals of the times.

The great Algonquin nation occupied the larger part of the Atlantic slope, the Valley of the St. Lawrence, and the country around the great lakes. It embraced the Pequods and Narragansetts of New England, the Micmacs of Nova Scotia, the Abenaquis of New Brunswick, the Montagnais and Ottawas of Quebec, the Ojibways or Chippewas on the great lakes, and the Crees and Sioux of the far West.

The Hurons and Iroquois were allied races, though for ages the most deadly enemies. They were more addicted to agriculture than the Algonquins, and dwelt in better houses, but they were equally fierce and implacable. The Hurons chiefly occupied the country between Lakes Erie, Ontario and Huron, and the northern banks of the St. Lawrence. Their principal settlement, till well-nigh exterminated by the Iroquois, was between Lake Simcoe and the Georgian Bay.

The Iroquois, or Five Nations, occupied northern

New York, from the Mohawk River to the Genesee.
The Confederacy embraced the Mohawks, Oneidas,
Onondagas, Cayugas, and Senecas, and was afterwards

INDIAN TYPE—FEATHER HEAD DRESS.

joined by the Tuscaroras from south Carolina. Each
tribe, however, asserted its independence, and made
war or peace on its own account, as was shown by

many a cruel raid upon Montreal or Quebec in a time
of nominal truce with the Confederacy. They were
the most cruel and blood-thirsty of all the savage
tribes—skilful in war, cunning in policy, and ruthless
in slaughter. They were chiefly the allies of the
British, and proved a thorn in the side of the French
for a hundred and fifty years. The latter, through
their missions, early acquired an ascendency over the
Algonquin and Huron tribes.

After the British conquest of Canada, the Indians
were gathered into Reserves, under military superin-
tendents, at Caughnawaga, the Bay of Quinte, Grand
River, Credit River, Rice Lake, River Thames,
Manitoulin and Walpole Islands, and elsewhere. They
were supplied with annual presents of knives, guns,
ammunition, blankets, trinkets, grain, implements,
and the like. Special efforts have been made, with
marked success, for their education in religion,
agricultural industry, and secular learning. Many
tribes have been raised from barbarism to Christian
civilization, although a few of the old men cling to
the faith of their fathers, and worship the Great
Spirit, beat the conjuror's drum, and sacrifice the
white dog. The Reserves are under the charge of an
Indian agent, who watches over the interests of the
tribe, and prevents the alienation of its property.

In the new Provinces of Manitoba and Keewatin
and in the North-West Territory are numerous tribes
of Plain or Forest Indians, for whom civilization has
as yet done little. They subsist chiefly by fishing and
collecting peltries for the Hudson's Bay Company

and other fur traders.   Missionaries, both Protestant
and Roman Catholic, have, with self-denying zeal,
laboured for their spiritual welfare, and in many cases
with very considerable success.   Treaties have been
made with most of these tribes, and liberal land
Reserves secured to them.

The Indian tribes in the Pacific Province of British
Columbia are, for the most part, pagan and savage.
Those on the sea coast live principally by fishing, in
which they exhibit great dexterity.   They hollow out,
with much patient labour, huge canoes from a single
tree-trunk.   They also build large framed and bark-
covered lodges, which will accommodate several
families.   In front of these they will often erect a
lofty tree-trunk, carved into hideous, grotesque
representations of the human face and figure,
bedaubed with bright, crude pigments.

The annual report of the Department of Indian
Affairs shows that, according to the latest official
statistics, there are in the Dominion 99,717 Indians.
The religious classification of the Indians is given as
follows :

	Protestants.	Catholics.	Pagan.
Ontario....................	9,654	6,354	1,258
Quebec	496	6,744	4,539
Nova Scotia...........		2,129	....
New Brunswick.........		1,540	....
Prince Edward Island.		304	....
British Columbia..	6,327	9,768	9,523
Manitoba..................	4,927	1,327	3,083
North-West	3,871	3,183	7,217
Totals..............	25,366	31,449	25,720

All the rest are pagan or not classified.

Near Brantford is the old Indian settlement to
which the Mohawk Indians were removed from their

OLD INDIAN CHURCH, NEAR BRANTFORD, ONT.

original settlements on the Mohawk River at the
time of the Revolutionary War.   Here is situated the

oldest church in the province. Its history can be traced back to 1784. It is still occupied for public worship. It possesses a handsome communion service of beaten silver, presented by Queen Anne to the Indian chapel on the Mohawk River. Beneath the walls of the humble sanctuary repose the ashes of the Mohawk chief, Thayendinaga—Joseph Brant—who gallantly fought for the British through two bloody wars.

Other Indian Reserves have been created at several places, as Winnipeg, New Credit, Rice Lake, Rama, Walpole Island and elsewhere. On these Reserves the Indians have been trained in the arts of peace, and, to a limited extent, in the practice of agriculture. But they do not exhibit much self-reliance nor aptitude of self-support; and the very assistance given them by the Government and the missionary societies of the several churches has, to a large degree, kept them in a state of tutelage and wardship that is unfavourable to the development of hardy energy of character. Yet many have been reclaimed from a life of barbarism and savagery, and elevated to the dignity of men and to the fellowship of saints. Our small cut shows the trim aspect of the Indian village at the Credit River, where the Rev. Dr. Ryerson, when a young man, spent the first year of his Christian ministry. He expresses, in his private journal, his trepidation on being called from this ministration to preach to the cultured and intelligent people of the town of York. At Munsey, Morley, Red Deer, Fort Simpson and elsewhere in Canada are flourishing Indian schools, under the management of the Methodist Church.

Fort William, at the time when I first saw it, was about as unmilitary-looking a place as it is possible to conceive. Instead of bristling with ramparts and cannon, and frowning defiance at the world, it quietly nestled, like a child in its mother's

CHRISTIAN INDIAN VILLAGE, PORT CREDIT.

lap, at the foot of McKay's Mountain, which loomed up grandly behind it A picket fence surrounded eight or ten acres of land, within which were a large stone store-house, the residence of the Chief Factor, and several dwelling-houses for the employés. At a little distance was the Indian mission. A couple of rusty cannon were the only war-like indications

3

visible. Yet the aspect of the place was not always so peaceful. A strong stockade once surrounded the post, and stone block-houses furnished protection to its defenders. It was long the stronghold of the North-West Company, whence they waged vigorous war against the rival Hudson's Bay Company. In its grand banquet chamber the annual feasts and councils of the chief factors were held, and alliances formed with the Indian tribes. Thence were issued the decrees of the giant monopoly which exercised a sort of feudal sovereignty from Labrador to Charlotte's Sound, from the United States boundry to Russian America. Thither came the plumed and painted sons of the forest to barter their furs for the knives and guns of Sheffield and Birmingham, and the gay fabrics of Manchester and Leeds, and to smoke the pipe of peace with their white allies. Those days have passed away. Paint and plumes are seen only in the far interior, and the furs are mostly collected far from the forts by agents of the company.

Our engraving represents one of the typical Red River carts still in use among the half-breeds throughout the North-West. It is peculiar in being made entirely of wood. There is neither nail nor metal tire. The thing creaks horribly, and when a hundred of them or more were out for the fall hunt, the groaning of the caravan was something appalling. The harness, too, is entirely home-made and exceedingly primitive. By means of these carts much of the freighting to the scattered forts of the North-West was done. It used to take ninety days for a brigade

to go from the Red River to Fort Edmonton. The
adhesive character of Winnipeg mud is indicated, for
these "antediluvian" carts are still occasionally seen
in the prairie capital, and it is a tribute to the strength
of the cart that the viscous material does not drag it
to pieces. The new arrivals can always be known by

RED RIVER CART.

the manner in which they slip and slide about on the
muddy street crossings.

The great natural features of the magnificent North-
West Territory are often of surpassing beauty, and
sometimes of grand sublimity. The prairies spreading
like a shoreless ocean, and starred with vari-coloured
flowers—flashing dew-crowned in the rosy light of

dawn, sleeping beneath the fervid blaze of noon, or crimson-dyed in the ruddy glow of sunset—are exquisitely beautiful. At night, when the rolling waves of grass gleam in the pallid moonlight, like foam-crests on the sea, or when the far horizon flares with lurid flames, and dun-rolling smoke-clouds mount the sky, they become sublime. So pure and dry and bracing is the atmosphere, that the range of vision is vastly increased, all the senses seem exalted, and new life is poured through every vein.

As we sweep on and on, all day long and all night, and all next day and half the night, a sense of the vastness of this great prairie region—like the vastness of the sea—grows upon one with overwhelming force. The following lines of Bryant's well describe some of the associations of a first view of the prairies :—

" These are the gardens of the Desert, these
    The unshorn fields, boundless and beautiful,
    For which the speech of England has no name—
    The Prairies. I behold them for the first,
    And my heart swells, while the dilated sight
    Takes in the encircling vastness. Lo ! they lie
    In airy undulations, far away,
    As if the ocean, in his gentlest swell,
    Stood still, with all his rounded billows fixed
    And motionless forever.—Motionless ?—
    No—they are all unchained again. The clouds
    Sweep over with their shadows, and, beneath,
    The surface rolls and fluctuates to the eye.
    Man hath no part in all this glorious work :
    The hand that built the firmament hath heaved
    And smoothed these verdant swells, and sown their slopes
    With herbage. .   .   .   The great heavens

Seem to stoop down upon the scene in love,—
A nearer vault, and of a tenderer blue,
Than that which bends above the eastern hills. . . .
In these plains the bison feeds no more, where once he shook
The earth with thundering steps—yet here I meet
His ancient footprints stamped beside the pool.

THE FUR TRADE.

Few of the dainty dames of London or Paris, or
even of Toronto or Montreal, have any conception of
the vicissitudes of peril and hardship encountered in
procuring the costly ermines and sables in which they
defy the winter's cold. About the month of August
the Indians of the great North-West procure a supply
of pork, flour and ammunition, generally on trust, at
the Hudson's Bay posts, and thread their way up the
lonely rivers and over many a portage, far into the
interior. There they build their bark lodges, generally
each family by itself, or sometimes a single individual
alone, scores of miles from his nearest neighbour.
They carry a supply of steel traps, which they carefully set and bait, concealing all appearance of design.
The hunter makes the round of his traps, often many
miles apart, returning to the camp, as by an unerring
instinct, through the pathless wilderness. The skins,
which are generally those of the otter, beaver, marten,
mink and sable, and occasionally of an Arctic fox or
bear, are stretched and dried in the smoke of the
wigwams. The trappers live chiefly on rabbits,
musk-rats, fish, and sometimes on cariboo, which they
hunt on snow-shoes. The loneliness of such a life is

appalling.   On every side stretches for hundreds of leagues the forest primeval.

Yet, to many there is a fascination in these solitudes. Lord Milton and Dr. Cheadle spent the winter of 1863-64 in a trapper's camp with great apparent enjoyment. Their provisions becoming exhausted, they had to send six hundred miles to Fort Garry, by a dog team, for four bags of flour and a few pounds of tea. The lonely trapper, however, must depend on his own resources.   In the spring he returns to the trading-posts, shooting the rapids of the swollen streams, frequently with bales of furs worth several hundreds of dollars. A sable skin which may be held in the folded hand is worth in the market of Europe $30 or $35, or of the finest quality $75. The Indians of the interior are models of honesty. They will not trespass on each other's streams or hunting-grounds, and always punctually repay the debt they have incurred at the trading-post. A Hudson's Bay store contains a miscellaneous assortment of goods, comprising such diverse articles as snow-shoes and cheap jewellery, canned fruit and blankets, gun-powder and tobacco, fishing-hooks and scalping-knives, vermilion for war-paint, and beads for embroidery. Many thousand dollars' worth of valuable furs are often collected at these posts. They are generally deposited in a huge log storehouse, and defended by a stockade, sometimes loopholed for musketry, or mounting a few small cannon. On the flag-staff is generally displayed the flag of the Company, with the strange motto, "*Pro pelle cutem,"*—Skin for skin. These posts are sparsely scattered over this vast territory. They are like oases in the wilderness, generally having a patch of cultivated ground, a garden of European plants and flowers, and all the material comforts of civilization. Their social isolation is the most objectionable feature. At one which I visited the Chief Factor had just sent one hundred and thirty miles in an open boat for the nearest physician. Yet, many of the factors are well educated men, who have changed the busy din of Glasgow or Edinburgh for the solitude of these far-off posts. And for love's sweet sake, refined and well-born women will abandon the luxuries of civilization to share the loneliness of the wilderness with their bosom's lord. One of the Hudson's Bay factors on Rupert's River wooed and won a fair Canadian girl, and took her back in triumph to his home. She was carried like an Indian princess over the portages and through the forests in a canoe, supported by cushions, wrapped in richest furs, and attended ever by a love that would not

> " Beteem the winds of heaven
> Visit her face too roughly."

There, in the heart of the wilderness, she kept her state and wore her jewels as if a queen of society.

Almost the sole method of exploring the great Northern fur regions is by means of the bark canoe in summer, or the dog-sledge or on snow-shoe in winter.

CANOE LIFE.

"The canoe," says Mr. H. M. Robinson, "is part of the savage. After generations of use, it has grown into the economy of his life. What the horse is to the Arab, the camel to the desert traveller, or the dog

MAKING A PORTAGE.

to the Esquimaux, the birch-bark canoe is to the Indian. The forests along the river shores yield all the materials requisite for its construction: Cedar for its ribs, birch bark for its outer covering, the thews of the juniper to sew together the separate pieces, and red pine to give resin for the seams and crevices.

" ' All the forest]life, is in it—
All its mystery and magic,
All the lightness of the birch-tree,
All the toughness of the cedar,
All the larch tree's supple sinews,
And it floated on the river
Like a yellow leaf in autumn,
Like a yellow water-lily.'

" During the summer season the canoe is the home of the red man. It is not only a boat, but a house; he turns it over him as a protection when he camps; he carries it long distances overland from lake to lake. Frail beyond words, yet he loads it down to the water's edge. In it he steers boldly out into the broadest lake, or paddles through wood and swamp and reedy shallow. Sitting in it he gathers his harvest of wild rice, or catches fish, or steals upon his game; dashes down the wildest rapid, braves the foaming torrent, or lies like a wild bird on the placid waters. While the trees are green, while the waters dance and sparkle, and the wild duck dwells in the sedgy ponds, the birch-bark canoe is the red man's home.

"And how well he knows the moods of the river! To guide his canoe through some whirling eddy, to shoot some roaring waterfall, to launch it by the edge of some fiercely-rushing torrent, or dash down a foaming rapid, is to be a brave and skilful Indian. The man who does all this, and does it well, must possess a rapidity of glance, a power in the sweep of his paddle, and a quiet consciousness of skill, not obtained save by long years of practice.

"An exceedingly light and graceful craft is the birch-bark canoe; a type of speed and beauty. So light that one man can easily carry it on his shoulders overland where a waterfall obstructs his progress; and as it only sinks five or six inches in the water, few places are too shallow to float it. In this frail bark, which measures anywhere from twelve to forty feet long, and from two to five feet broad in the middle, the Indian and his family travel over the innumerable lakes and rivers, and the fur-hunters pursue their lonely calling.

"Frequently the ascent of the streams is not made without mishap. Sometimes the canoe runs against a stone, and tears a small hole in the bottom. This obliges the voyagers to put ashore immediately and repair the damage. They do it swiftly and with admirable dexterity. Into the hole is fitted a piece of bark; the fibrous roots of the pine tree sew it in its place, and the place pitched, so as to be water-tight, all within an hour. Again, the current is too strong to admit of the use of paddles, and recourse is had to poling, if the stream be shallow, or tracking if the depth of water forbid the use of poles. The latter is an extremely toilsome process, and detracts much from the romance of canoe-life in the wilderness. Tracking, as it is called, is dreadfully harassing work. Half the crew go ashore and drag the boat slowly along while the other half go asleep. After an hour's walk the others take their turn, and so on, alternately, during the entire day.

"But, if the rushing or breasting up a rapid is

exciting, the operation of shooting them in a birch-
bark canoe is doubly so.   True, all the perpendicular falls have to be "portaged," and in a day's
journey of forty miles, from twelve to fifteen
portages have to be made.   But the rapids are as
smooth water to the hardy voyagers, who, in anything less than a perpendicular fall, seldom lift the
canoe from the water.   As the frail birch-bark canoe
nears the rapid from above, all is quiet.   The most
skilful voyager sits on his heels in the bow of the
canoe, the next best oarsman similarly placed in the
stern.   The hand of the bowsman becomes a living
intelligence as, extended behind him, it motions the
steersman where to turn the craft.   The latter never
takes his eye off that hand for an instant.   Its
varied expression becomes the life of the canoe.

"The bowsman peers straight ahead with a glance
like that of an eagle.   The canoe, seeming like a
cockle-shell in its frailty, silently approaches the
rim where the waters disappear from view.   On
the very edge of the slope the bowsman suddenly
stands up, and, bending forward his head, peers
eagerly down the eddying rush, then falls upon his
knees again.   Without turning his head for an
instant, the hand behind him signals its warning to
the steersman.   Now there is no time for thought;
no eye is quick enough to take in the rushing scene.
There are strange currents, unexpected whirls, and
backward eddies and rocks—rocks rough and jagged,
smooth, slippery and polished—and through all this
the canoe glances like an arrow, dips like a wild bird

SHOOTING A RAPID

down the wing of the storm. All this time not a word is spoken; but every now and again there is a quick twist of the bow paddle to edge far off some rock, to put her full through some boiling billow, to hold her steady down the slope of some thundering chute.

"But the old canoe-life of the Fur Land is rapidly passing away. In many a once well-beaten pathway, naught save narrow trails over the portages, and rough wooded crosses over the graves of travellers who perished by the way, remains to mark the roll of the passing years."

The Indians near the frontier settlements, who hang upon the skirts of civilization, are not favourable specimens of their race. They acquire the white man's vices rather than his virtues. They are a squalid, miserable set; their bark wigwams are filthy, comfortless structures. The older women are horribly withered, bleared, and smoke-dried creatures, extremely suggestive of the witches in "Macbeth." The younger squaws are very fond of supplementing their savage costume with gay ribbons, beads, and other civilized finery; and in one wigwam I saw a crinoline skirt hanging up. The men are often idle, hulking fellows. They keep a great number of dogs—vile curs of low degree; and in one camp which I visited was an exceedingly tame raven. Neither sex commonly wears any head-dress in summer, save the coarse hair hanging in a tangled mass over the eyes. The food supply is often extremely precarious. Anything more wretched than the dependence for subsistence on the fish caught through the ice on the lakes and streams in winter is hard to conceive. In the days when buffalo were plenty the great fall hunt was a time of reckless feasting on buffaloes' tongues. The tenderest portions were dried in the air and often manufactured into pemmican—that is, the dried flesh was broken into fine pieces and pressed into a skin bag, and over it was poured melted tallow. This extremely strong and wholesome food was long a staple at all the Hudson's Bay Company's forts.

Indian Missions.

In the far interior, where the Indians are removed from the baleful influence of the white man's firewater, a finer type exists. The Hudson's Bay Company has always sedulously excluded that bane of the red race wherever their jurisdiction extends. Among the protégés of the company, therefore, Christian missions have had their greatest successes, although their nomad life almost negatives every attempt to civilize them. Near many of the posts is a Jesuit mission, frequently a heritage from the times of French supremacy. There are a number of Church of England missions, generally near the settlements, and some very successful Presbyterian missions. The Indian missions of the Methodist Church are, however, more numerous than those of any other body, and have been attended with very great success. It has in the Dominion (in 1894), chiefly in Hudson's Bay Territory, fifty Indian missions, 4,612 communicants, and probably 15,000 members of congregation. Many of these, once pagan savages, now adorn with their lives their profession of the Gospel.

There are no more arduous mission fields in the world than those among the native tribes of the great North-West. The devoted servant of the Cross goes forth to a region beyond the pale of civilization. He often suffers privation of the very necessaries of life. He is exposed to the rigour of an almost Arctic winter. He is cut off from human sympathy or congenial companionship. Communication with the great world is often maintained by infrequent and irregular mails, conveyed by long and tortuous canoe routes in summer or on dog-sleds in winter. The unvarnished tales of some of these missionaries lack no feature of heroic daring and apostolic zeal. But recently one, with his newly-wedded wife, a lady of much culture and refinement, travelled hundreds of miles by lake and river, often making toilsome portages, once in danger of their lives by the up-setting of their birch-bark canoe in an arrowy rapid. In midwinter the same intrepid missionary made a journey of several hundred miles in a dog-sled, sleeping in the snow with the thermometer forty, and even fifty, degrees below zero, in order to open a new mission among a pagan tribe !

WINTER TRAVEL.

In winter the snow falls deep and is packed hard by the wind. To walk well on snow, there is nothing

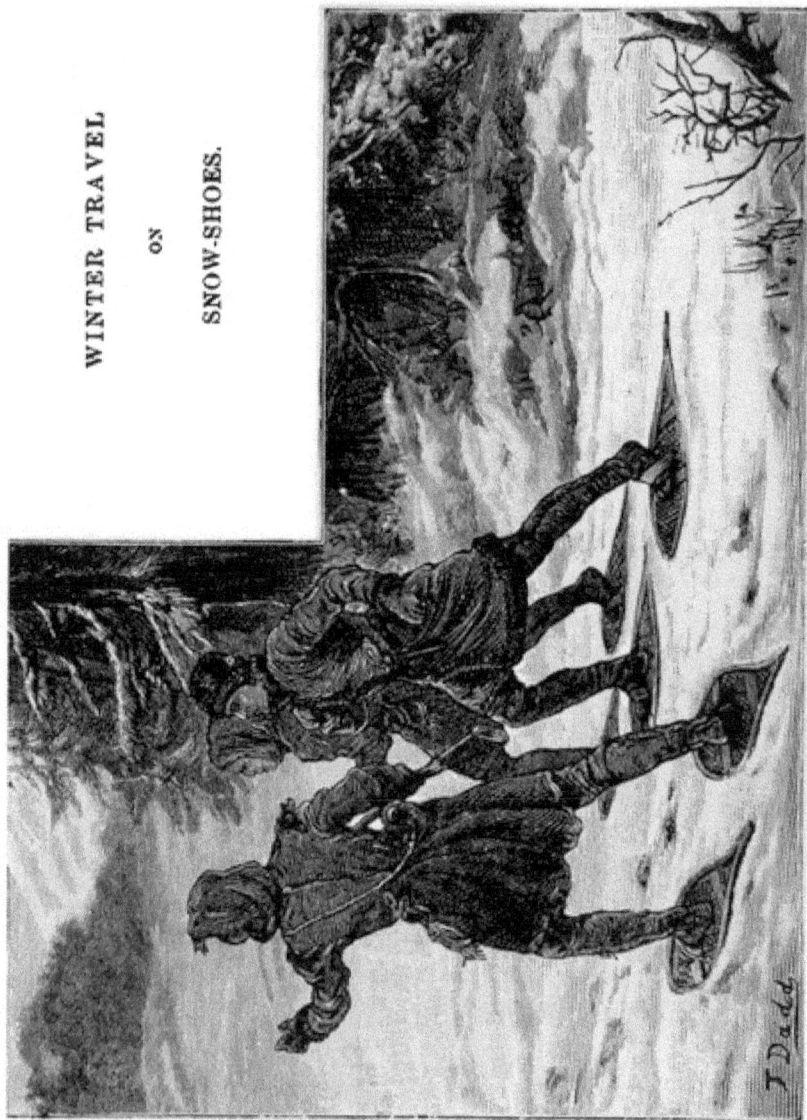

WINTER TRAVEL

ON

SNOW-SHOES.

like snow-shoes. These are composed of a light
wooden frame about four feet in length, tapering from
a width of about fifteen inches at the centre to points
at either end, the toes being turned up so as to prevent tripping. Over this frame a netting of deer-skin
sinews or threads is stretched for the foot of the runner
to rest upon. The object of this appliance is by a thin
network to distribute the weight of the wearer over
so large a surface of snow as will prevent him from
sinking. The credit of the invention is due to the
Indians, and, like that of the canoe and other Indian
instruments, it is so perfectly suited to the object in
view as not to be susceptible of improvement by the
whites.

On snow-shoes an Indian or half-breed will travel
thirty, forty, and sometimes even fifty miles in twenty-
four hours. It is the common and, indeed, the only
available mode of foot-travel away from the public
highways in winter.

Travelling otherwise than on foot is accomplished
almost entirely by means of dogs. The following
account of winter travel is taken from H. M. Robinson's graphic book on "The Great Fur Land": "The
vehicles to which the dogs are harnessed are of three
kinds—the passenger sledge or dog-cariole, the freight
sledge, and the travaille. A cariole consists of a very
thin board, usually not over half an inch thick, fifteen
to twenty inches wide, and about ten feet long, turned
up at one end in the form of a half circle, like a
toboggan. To this board a light frame-work box is
attached, about eighteen inches from the rear end.

4

When travelling it is lined with buffalo-robes and blankets, in the midst of which the passenger sits, or rather reclines; the vehicle being prevented from capsizing by the driver, who runs behind on snow-shoes, holding on to a line attached to the back part of the cariole. The projecting end or floor behind the passenger's seat is utilized as a sort of boot upon which to tie baggage, or as a platform upon which the driver may stand to gain a temporary respite when tired of running. Four dogs to each sledge form a complete train. They are harnessed to the cariole by means of two long traces.

"The rate of speed usually attained in sledge-travel is about forty miles per day of ten hours, although this rate is often nearly doubled. Four miles an hour is a common dog-trot when the animals are well loaded; but this can be greatly exceeded when hauling a cariole containing a single passenger upon smooth snow-crust or a beaten track. Very frequently extra-ordinary distances are compassed by a well-broken train of dogs. Sixty or eighty miles per day is not infrequently made in the way of passenger travel. An average train of four dogs will trot briskly along with three hundred pounds' weight without difficulty."

Our engraving on next page shows the Rev. Egerton Ryerson Young, for nine years a missionary in the North-West, in winter costume. Writing of this picture, Mr. Young says:

"My own appearance will seem rather peculiar and unministerial. However, it is just about as I gener-ally looked when working or travelling in the winter

REV. E. R. YOUNG IN TRAVELLING DRESS.

in that cold land, where the spirit thermometer—for
the mercury would often be frozen—used to get down
to from forty to fifty degrees below zero.   The suit is
of leather—dressed moose skin, or reindeer skin—
trimmed with fur.   The Indian women, who make
these leather suits, trim them also with a great deal
of deer-skin fringe.   In their wild state on the plains,
the warlike Indians used to have these fringes made
of the scalps of their enemies."

In the foreground is the famous dog "Jack," a huge
St. Bernard, given Mr. Young by the Hon. Senator
Sanford, of Hamilton.   He more than once, by his
sagacity and strength, saved the missionary's life.

Mr. Young thus describes a winter journey in the
North Land :

" Ere we start let us examine our outfit—our dogs,
our Indians, our sleds and their loads.   The dogs are
called the Esquimo or ' Huskie' dog.   I used them
altogether on my long winter journeys until I imported
my St. Bernards and Newfoundlands.   These Esquimo
dogs are queer fellows.   Their endurance is wonderful,
their tricks innumerable, their appetites insatiable,
their thievish propensities unconquerable.   It seems
to be their nature to steal, and they never get the
mastery of it.

" Off we go.   How the dogs seem to enjoy the sport.
With heads and tails up they bark and bound along as
though it were the greatest fun.   The Indians, too,
are full of life, and are putting in their best paces.
The bracing air and vigorous exercise make us very
hungry, and about noon we will stop and dine.   A

few small dry trees are cut down and a fire is quickly
built. Snow is soon melted, tea is made, and this,
with some boiled meat and biscuits, will do very well.
Our axes and kettles are again fastened to the sleds,
and we are off again. We journey on until the sun
is sinking in the West, and the experienced Indian
guide says we will need all the daylight that is left in
which to prepare our camp for the night.

"Of our Indian runners it is a great pleasure to
speak. Faithfully, indeed, were their services rendered, and bright are the memories of their untiring
devotion and constancy. When their feet and ours
were bleeding and nearly every footprint of our trail
was marked with blood, their cheerfulness never
failed them, and their hearts quailled not. When supplies ran short, and home and plenty were many days
distant, can we ever forget how, ere the missionary
was made aware of the emptiness of the provision
bags, they so quietly put themselves on quarter
rations that there might yet be sufficient full meals
for him? And then, when the long day's journey of
perhaps sixty or eighty miles was ended, and we
gathered at our camp fire, with no roof above us but
the stars, no friendly shelter within scores of miles
of us, how kindly, and with what reverence and
respect, did they enter into the worship of the great
God who had shielded us from so many dangers, and
brought us to that hour. Sometimes they tried our
patience, for they were human and so were we; but
much more frequently they won our admiration by
their marvellous endurance, and unerring skill and

wisdom in trying hours, when blizzards raged and blinding snow-storms obliterated all traces of the trail, and 'the white man became so confused and affected by the cold that he was hardly able to distinguish his right hand from his left

DOG TEAMS.

" Picturesque was their costume, as in new leather suites, gaily adorned with bead or porcupine quilt work, by the skilful hand of bright-eyed wife or mother, they were on hand to commence the long journey. And when the 'Farewells,' to loved ones were said, and the word 'Marche!' was given, how rapid was their pace, and how marvellous their ability to keep it up for many a long, long day. To the missionary they were ever loyal and true. Looking over nine years of faithful service to him, as he went up and down through the dreary wastes preaching Jesus, often where His name had never been heard before, he cannot recall a single instance of treachery or ingratitude, but many of devoted attachment and unselfish love. Some of them have since finished the long journey, and have entered in through the gate into the celestial city about which they loved to hear us talk as we clustered round the camp fire. May we all get there by-and-by.

"One of the most remarkable fruits of missionary labour among the aborigines was the native missionsionary, Henry B. Steinhaur, whose portrait we give on page 58. He was an Ojibway Indian, born on the Rama Reserve, in 1820, and trained in the Indian School at Grape Island. He afterwards received a liberal education at Victoria College. In 1840 he went as a missionary to his red brethren in the far North-West, paddling his own canoe for hundreds of miles to reach his future field of labour. He translated large portions of the Scriptures and hymn-book into the native dialect. In 1854 he accompanied the Rev. John Ryerson to Great Britain, and pleaded eloquently the cause of his red brethren before the British Churches. He again devoted himself to missionary toil in the North-West, travelling with native tribes on their hunts, and planting among them the germs of Christian civilization. After a life of earnest toil for their evangelization, he passed from

labour to reward on the last Sunday of 1884, leaving
two sons to walk in their father's footsteps as missionaries to the aboriginal races of the North-West.

"Our cut on page 60," says Mr. Young, "gives an

HENRY B. STEINHAUR.

idea of what a winter camp in those northern regions is, under the most favourable circumstances. To get away from the fierce breezes that so often blow on the lake, we turn into the forest, perhaps a quarter of a mile. The first thing done after finding a suitable place for the camp is to unharness the dogs. Then, using our big snow-shoes as shovels, we clear away the snow from a level spot, where we build up our camp fire, around which we spend the night. Our camp kettles are got out and supper is prepared. Then balsam boughs are cut and are spread on the ground under our robes and blankets, adding much to our comfort. Our dogs must not be forgotten, and so frozen fish in sufficient numbers are taken from our sleds to give a couple to each dog. As these are frozen as hard almost as stones we thaw them out at the fire, What a pleasure it used to be to feed the dogs! How they did enjoy their only meal of the whole day! What appetites they had! The way those dogs could eat twelve or fourteen pounds of white fish, and then come and ask for more, was amazing.

"There was some dogs that seemed always hungry, and never would be quiet. All night long they kept prowling round in the camp among the kettles, or over us while we tried to sleep. They were very jealous of each other when in camp, and as they passed and repassed each other it was ever with a snarl. Sometimes it would result in open war, and we have more than once been rudely aroused from our slumbers by finding eight or ten dogs fighting for

CAMPING OUT IN THE SNOW IN THE NORTH-WEST.

what seemed to be the honour of sleeping on our heads."

The fatigue of travelling in the benumbing cold, perhaps with a keen wind blowing over the icy lake, cannot be adequately described. Sometimes a "blizzard" would prevent travel altogether, and drive the missionary to seek shelter. Mr. Young exclaims: "How we used to enjoy the wintry camp after a fatiguing day's journey, when both missionary and Indians had tramped all day on snow-shoes. It was a real luxury to find a place where we could sit down and rest our aching bones and tired and often bleeding feet. With plenty of dry wood and good food we forgot our sorrows and our isolation, and our morning and evening devotions were filled with gratitude and thankfulness to the great Giver of all good for His many mercies.

"How gloriously the stars shone out in those northern skies, and how brilliant were the meteors that flashed athwart the heavens! But the glory of that land, surpassing any and every other sight that this world affords, is the wondrous Aurora. Never alike, and yet always beautiful, it breaks the monotonous gloom of those long, dismal wintry nights, with ever-changing splendour. The arc of light is visible sometimes in the northern sky as we see it here; then it would become strangely agitated, and would deluge us in floods of light. Sometimes at the zenith a glorious corona would be formed that flashed and scintillated with such brilliancy that the eye was pained with its brightness. Suddenly bars of col-

WAR DANCE IN THE SKY.

The Indians imagine that they can see in the Northern
Lights warlike figures dancing in the sky.

oured light shot out from it, reaching down apparently to the shore afar off. The pagan Indians, as with awe-struck countenances they gazed upon some of these wonderful sights, said they were spirits of their war-like ancestors going out to battle. A great many of them are no longer pagans. Through numerous difficulties and hardships the missionaries have gone to them with the story of the Cross, and hundreds of these once savage men are devout followers of the Lord Jesus. Their conversion to Christianity has amply repaid the missionaries for all they have suffered in the bitter cold winters, when, with dog trains, they were obliged to journey scores or even hundreds of miles to carry to them the news of salvation. But there are many yet unconverted, and, thank God, there are devoted missionaries still willing to suffer and endure the bitter cold if, by so doing, they can bring them into the fold of the Good Shepherd."

Another local superstition is that of the Giant of Lake Winnipeg—a mysterious being, who, at the witching hour of night, guides his strange craft swiftly on the bright moonlit pathway on the lake, and as mysteriously disappears. It is customary to place offerings of tobacco, etc., as a peace-offering on a rock by the lake side.

Norway House is a large establishment of the Hudson's Bay Company, twenty miles north of the northern extremity of Lake Winnipeg. It was for many years one of the most important of all the company's posts. Gentlemen of the company and large numbers of Indians used to gather here every summer, some of them coming from vast distances. The furs of half a continent almost were here collected, and then sent down to York Factory on the Hudson's Bay, and from that place shipped to England.

Rossville Mission is two miles from Norway House. This mission is one of the most flourishing in the wild North Land.   Here it was that the Rev. James Evans invented the wonderful syllabic characters for the Cree Indians. In these characters the whole Bible is now printed, as well as a large number of hymns and catechisms. So simple is the system that an average Indian can learn to read in three or four days.   The church at Rossville is large, and is often filled with hundreds of Indians, who love to hear the Word of God.

"That human beings can live in such frail bark wigwams," says Mr. Young, "in such cold regions is, indeed, surprising. But they do, and many of them seem to thrive amazingly. Many a stormy day and night I have spent in those queer dwelling-places. Sometimes the winds whistled and fine snow drifted in through the many openings between the layers of the birch bark, of which they were generally made, and I shivered until my teeth rattled again. Often the smoke from the little fire, built on the ground in the centre of the tent, refused to ascend and go out through the top; then my eyes suffered, and tears would unbidden start. What a mixed-up crowd we often were. Men, women, children, and dogs—and

PLAIN INDIAN CAMP.

all smoking except the missionary and the dogs. During the day we huddled around the fire in a circle with our feet tucked in under us. After supper, and when the prayers were over, we each wrapped our blanket around us and stretched ourselves out with our feet toward the fire, like the spokes of a wheel, the fire in the centre representing the hub. Frequently the wigwam was so small that we dare not stretch out our feet for fear of putting them in the fire, and so had to sleep in a position very much like a half-opened jack-knife."

In the prairie region the tepees are generally made of skins, as shown in the cut. These are much warmer and more comfortable than the birch-bark wigwams

The mode of disposing of the dead is very remarkable. In some places the bodies are put in rude caskets or wrapped in skins or blankets and placed in trees. The Plain Indians erect a scaffold on the prairie, on which reposes the dead body out of the reach of the coyote or prairie wolf.

Few records of self-sacrifice are more sublime than that of the devoted band at Edmonton House, near the Rocky Mountains, ministering with Christ-like tenderness and pity to the Indians smitten with that loathsome scourge, the small-pox. Few pictures of bereavement are more pathetic than that of the survivors, themselves enfeebled through disease, laying in their far-off lonely graves their loved ones who fell martyrs to their pious zeal. For these plumeless heroes of the Christian chivalry all human praise is cold and meagre; but the "Well done!" of the Lord they loved is their exceeding great reward.

The heroic McDougalls, father and sons, will be forever associated in the annals of missionary heroism
throughout the North-West. The elder McDougall
was a pathfinder of Empire as well as a pioneer of
Christianity. After many years spent in preaching
the Gospel to the native tribes he died a tragic death,
but one not unfitting the heroism of his life. While
out on a hunting excursion with his sons he became
lost on the prairie, and not till after several days was
his frozen body found wrapped in icy sleep beneath
the wintry sky. His missionary son walks with
equal zeal in the footsteps of his sainted sire, and
during the late North-West revolt rendered important
service in assisting to pacify the restive Indian tribes.
These and other Indian missionaries often assumed
the native dress, as in our engraving, which was comfortable, enduring and well fitted to resist the wear
and tear of their lengthened travels and hard work.

Few spectacles are more sad than that of the decay
of the once numerous and powerful native tribes that
inhabited these vast regions. The extinction of the
race in the not very remote future seems to be its
probable destiny. Such has already been the fate of
portions of the great aboriginal family. In the
library of Harvard University, near Boston, is an old
and faded volume, which, nevertheless, possesses an
intensely pathetic interest. In all the world there is
none who comprehends the meaning of its mysterious
characters. It is a sealed book and its voice is silent
forever. Yet its language was once the vernacular
of a numerous and powerful tribe. But of those who

spoke that tongue there runs no kindred drop of blood in any human veins. It is the Bible, translated for the use of the New England Indians by Eliot, the great apostle of their race.

INDIAN MISSIONARY.

That worn and meagre volume, with its speechless pages, is the symbol of a mighty fact. Like the bones of the mammoth and the mastodon, it is the relic of an extinct creation. It is the only vestige of a vanished race—the tombstone over the grave of a nation. And similar to the fate of the New England Indians seems to be the doom of the entire aboriginal population of this continent. They are melting away like winter snows before the summer's sun. Their inherent character is averse to the genius of modern civilization. You cannot mew up the eagle of the mountain like the barn-door fowl, nor tame the forest stag like the stalled ox. So to the red man the trammels and fetters of civilized life are irksome. They chafe his very soul. Like the caged eagle, he pines for the freedom of the forest or the prairie. He now stalks a stranger through the heritage of his fathers—an object of idle curiosity, where once he was Lord of the soil. He dwells not in our cities. He assimilates not with our habits. He lingers among us in scattered Reserves, or hovers upon the frontier of civilization, ever pushed back by its advancing tide. To our remote descendants the story of the Indian tribes will be a dim tradition, as that of the Celts and Picts and ancient Britons is to us. Already their arrow-heads and tomahawks are collected in our museums as strange relics of a bygone era. Our antiquarians, even now, speculate with a puzzled interest on their memorial mounds and burrows with feelings akin to those excited by the pyramids of Gizeh, or the megaliths of Stonehenge.

We, of the white race, are in the position of warders to these weak and perishing tribes.   They look up to our beloved Sovereign as their "Great Mother."   We are their elder and stronger brethren—their natural protectors and guardians.   The Government, it is true, has exercised a paternal care over the Indians, It has gathered them into Reserves, and bestowed upon them annual gifts and pensions.   But the white man's civilization has brought more of bane than of blessing.   His vices have taken root more deeply than his virtues; and the diseases he has introduced have, at times, threatened the extermination of the entire race.

Many whole tribes have, through the influence of the missionaries, become Christianized, and many individuals, as John Sunday and Peter Jones, have become distinguished advocates of their race, who have pleaded their cause with pathetic eloquence on public platforms in Great Britain.   One of the ablest of these civilized Indians was Chief Joseph Brant, whose portrait we give.   He was distinguished for his unswerving loyalty to the British, and gallantly fought for king and country during two bloody wars.

Many of these tribes are still pagan, and sacrifice the white dog, worship the great Manitou, and are the prey of cunning medicine-men and of super-stitious fears.   Others give an unintelligent observance to the ritual of a ceremonial form of Christianity, and regard the Cross only as a more potent fetish than their ancestral totem.   As the white race has, in

many respects, taught them to eat of the bitter fruit
of the tree of knowledge of good and evil, be it theirs

TYENDINAGA— CHIEF JOSEPH BRANT.

to pluck for them the healing leaves of the tree of
life! As they have occupied their ancient inherit-

ance, be it theirs to point them to a more enduring
country, an inheritance incorruptible and undefiled
—fairer fields and lovelier plains than even the fabled
hunting-grounds of their fathers—

> "In the kingdom of Ponomah,
> In the region of the West wind,
> In the land of the Hereafter."

WINNIPEG.

The strongest impression made upon the tourist on
his first visit to Winnipeg is one of amazement that
so young a city should have made such wonderful
progress. Its public buildings, and many of its
business blocks and private residences, exhibit a
solidity and magnificence of which any city in the
Dominion might be proud. The engraving on page
73 gives a view of this now thriving city as it
appeared in 1872, while the one on page 75 shows
the marvellous progress made in twelve years. It is
already an important railway centre, from which
seven or eight railways issue ; and it is evidently destined to be one of the most important distributing
points for a vast extent of the most fertile country
in the world.

The broad block-paved Main Street of Winnipeg,
twice as wide as the average street in Toronto, with
its bustling business and attractive stores, is a
genuine surprise. Its magnificent new City Hall
surpasses in the elegance of its architecture any
other that I know in Canada. The new Post Office
is a very handsome building, and the stately Cauchon

Block and Hudson's Bay Company's buildings in architecture and equipment and stock, seem to the visitor to have anticipated the possible wants of the

WINNIPEG IN 1872.

community by a score of years. Grace Church is very elegant and commodious within, but without looks like a great wholesale block. It was so constructed that when the permanent church, which it is proposed in time to erect, is built, the old one can be with ease converted into a large wholesale store.

It was with peculiar interest that I wandered over the site of the historic Fort Garry—now almost entirely obliterated. The old gateway and the old Governor's residence—a broad-eaved, solid, comfortable-looking building—and a few old store-houses are all that remain of the historic old fort which dominated the mid-continent, and from which issued commands which were obeyed throughout the vast regions reaching to the Rocky Mountains and the shores of Hudson's Bay. It has also its more recent stormy memories. Around the town may be seen numerous half-breeds and Indians. Of the latter we give cuts of characteristic types.

THROUGH THE NORTH-WEST TERRITORIES.

We resume our journey over the Canadian Pacific Railway at the western confines of Manitoba. The sun went down in crimson splendour, and during the night Broadview, Qu'Appelle, Regina, Moose Jaw, Swift Current, and a score of other places were passed. I must be dependent for an account of places passed by night on the excellent guide-book published by the Canadian Pacific Railway.

Regina is the capital of the Province of Assiniboia, and the distributing point for the country far north and south. The Executive Council of the North-West Territories, embracing the Provinces of Assiniboia, Alberta, Saskatchewan and Athabasca, meets

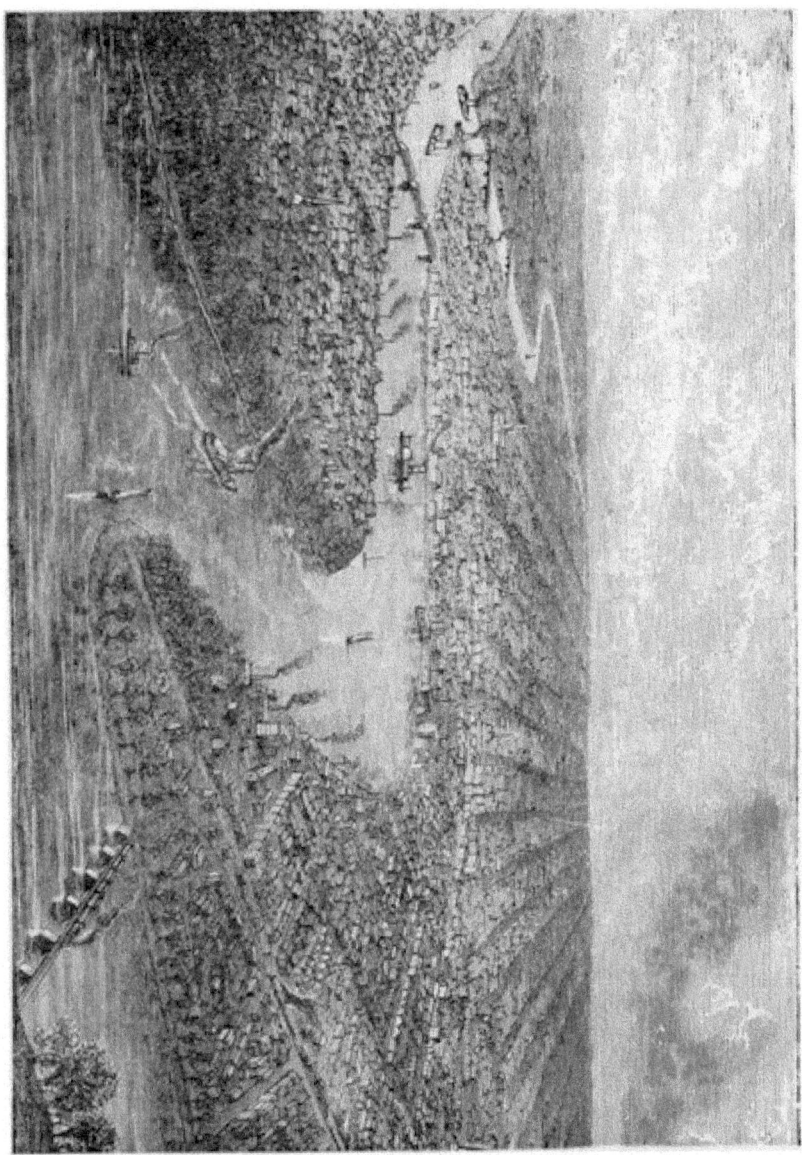

WYNANDS · TRANSVAAL

here, and the jurisdiction of the Lieutenant-Governor, whose residence is here, extends over all these provinces. The headquarters of the North-West Mounted Police, with the barracks, officers' quarters, offices, storehouses and the imposing drill-hall, together make a handsome village. Moose Jaw is a railway divisional point and a busy market town near the western limit of the present settlements. The name is an abridgment of the Indian name, which, literally translated, is "The-creek-where-the-white-man-mended-the-cart-with-moosejaw-bone." The country is treeless from the eastern border of the Regina plain to the Cypress Hills, two hundred miles, but the soil is excellent nearly everywhere, and the experimental farms of the railway company, which occur at intervals of thirty miles all the way to the mountains, have proved the sufficiency of the rainfall.

Next day the general features of the landscape continued still the same. The stations, however, are farther apart, and the settlers fewer in number. In some places the station-house is the only building in sight. At one such place, a couple of tourists came out on the platform as the train came to a stop.

Everywhere are evidences of the former presence of the countless herds of buffalo that pastured on these plains. Their deeply-marked trails—great grooves worn in the tough sod—show where they sought their favourite pastures, or salt licks, or drinking-places; and their bleaching skeletons whiten the ground where they lay down and died, or, more

likely, were ruthlessly slaughtered for the tongues
and skins. Their bones have been gathered near the
stations in great mounds—tons and tons of them—
and are shipped by the carload to the eastern cities,
for the manufacture of animal charcoal for sugar
refining. The utter extinction of the bison is one of
the most remarkable results of the advance of civilization. Ten years ago, in their migration from south
to north, they so obstructed the Missouri River,
where they crossed, that steamboats were compelled
to stop in mid-stream; and an eye-witness assured
me he could have walked across the river on the
animals' backs. Now scarce a buffalo is to be seen,
except in the far Valley of the Peace River, and a
score of half-domesticated ones near Winnipeg.

Among the interesting objects seen on the plains
are the remarkable little rodents known as prairie
dogs. They dig underground burrows with remarkable facility, at the mouth of which they will sit
with a cunning air of curiosity till something disturbs
them when, *presto*, a twinkling disappearing tail is
the last that is seen of them. It is said that rattle-
snakes and owls will occupy the same burrows, but
of that this deponent sayeth not. (See cut page 82.)

The presence of the Mounted Police is evidently a
terror to evil-doers, especially to whiskey smugglers
and horse-thieves. The police have a smart military
look, with their scarlet tunics, white helmets, spurred
boots, and riding trousers. Their arms are a repeat-
ing carbine and a six-shooter, with a belt of car-
tridges. They made a more than perfunctory search

FORT GARRY.

for liquor on the train; an Irish immigrant was very
indignant at this interference with the liberty of the
subject. A good deal of liquor was formerly smuggled
in barrels of sugar and the like, and some villainous
concoctions are still brought in by traders from the
American frontier. It is a glorious thing that
throughout so large an area of our country the liquor
traffic is under ban. God grant that these fresh and
virgin prairies may continue forever uncursed by
the blight of strong drink! The granting of permits,
however, gives frequent opportunities for evading the
prohibition.

At many of the stations a few Indians or half-
breeds may be seen, and sometimes the red man, with
painted face and feathers, brass ear-rings and necklace, and other savage finery. He is not a very
heroic figure, and the squaws look still worse. They
are generally wrapped in dirty blankets, and carry
their papooses tucked in at their backs. They sell
buffalo horns, from which the rough outer surface
had been chipped or filed off—the hard black core
being polished by the hand to a lustrous smoothness.
They exhibit only one pair at a time, and when that
is sold they jerk another pair, a little better, from
under their blankets.

As one rides day after day over the vast and fertile
prairies of the great North-West, he cannot help feeling
the question come home again and again to his mind
—What shall the future of these lands be? The
tamest imagination cannot but kindle at the thought
of the grand inheritance God has given to us and to

our children in this vast domain of empire. Almost
the whole of Europe, omitting Russia and Sweden,
might be placed within the prairie region of the
North-West; and a population greater than that of
Europe may here find happy homes. The prophetic
voice of the seer exclaims :

> I hear the tread of pioneers,
>   Of nations yet to be,
> The first low wash of waves, where soon
>   Shall roll a human sea.
>
> The rudiments of empire here
>   Are plastic yet and warm ;
> The chaos of a mighty world
>   Is rounding into form.
>
> Behind the scared squaw's birch canoe,
>   The steamer smokes and raves ;
> And city lots are staked for sale,
>   Above old Indian graves.

The child is now living who shall live to see great
provinces carved out of these North-West Territories,
and great cities strung like pearls along its iron roads
and water-ways. Now is the hour of destiny; now
is the opportunity to mould the future of this vast
domain—to lay deep and strong and staple the
foundations of the commonweal, in those Christian
institutions which shall be the corner-stone of our
national greatness.

To quote again from Whittier:

> We cross the prairie as of old
>   The pilgrims crossed the sea,
> To make the West as they the East
>   The homestead of the free !

We go to plant her common schools
  On distant prairie swells,
And give the Sabbaths of the wild
  The music of her bells.

Upbearing, like the ark of old,
  The Bible in our van,
We go to test the truth of God
  Against the fraud of man.

While other Churches have rendered immense service to Christianity and civilization in this vast region,
I am more familiar with the missionary work of the
Methodist Church. That Church has no cause to be
ashamed of its record in this heroic work. It has
been a pathfinder of Protestant missions throughout
the vast regions stretching from Nelson River to the
slopes of the Rocky Mountains. Nearly fifty years
ago, when these regions were less accessible than is
the heart of Africa to-day, those pioneer missionaries,
Rundle and Evans, planted the Cross and preached
the Gospel to the wandering Indians of the forest
and the plains. Nor have they been without their
heroic successors from that day to this.

The large number of Indians on the Pacific Coast
presents another important element in the missionary
problem in that country. Though by no means, as
a whole, a very high type of humanity, they are yet
much superior to the Indians of the plains whom I
saw. There is a little cove in Victoria harbour where
the boats of the West Coast Indians most do congre-
gate. These are large, strong canoes, each hewn out
of a single log. Many of them will carry a dozen

persons or more. In the National Museum at Washington is one from Alaska, over sixty feet long and five or six feet wide. In these they sail for hundreds of miles along the coast, fishing, sealing, and hunting, and bringing the result of their industry to Victoria

A HAPPY FAMILY—PRAIRIE DOGS, OWLS AND SNAKE.

for barter. The chief peril they encounter at sea is that their wooden craft may split from stem to stern through the force of the waves. These dug-outs are fantastically carved and painted. Several of them lay in the little cove just mentioned, their owners sound asleep or basking half awake in the sun. The

men have short squat figures and broad flat faces,
with a thick thatch of long black hair, both head and
feet being bare. The women wear bright party-
coloured shawls, and frequently a profusion of rings,
necklaces, and other cheap jewellery. I saw some with
rings in their nose and copper bracelets on their arms.
A little family group were roasting and eating mus-
sels on the rocks. A not uncomely Indian woman
gave me some. They were not at all unpalatable,
and if one only had some salt and bread, would make
a very good meal; but roast mussel alone was rather
unappetising fare. A pretty black-eyed child was
playing with a china doll, and another had a little
toy-rabbit. It is quite common to see these Indian
women squatting patiently on the sidewalk hour after
hour—time is a commodity of which they seem to
have any quantity at their disposal.

It is among these poor creatures, too often the prey
of the white man's vices and the victims of the white
man's diseases, that some of the most remarkable
missionary triumphs on this continent have been
achieved. The totem poles shown in one of our
engravings are not the "idols" of the Indian tribes,
as has been asserted, but their family crests. The
Indians have quite a heraldry of their own, and some
of the carvings are certainly as grotesque as any of
the dragons, griffins or wyverns of the Garter-King-
at-Arms.

Few things exhibit stronger evidence of the trans-
forming power of divine grace than the contrast
between the Christian life and character of the con-

6

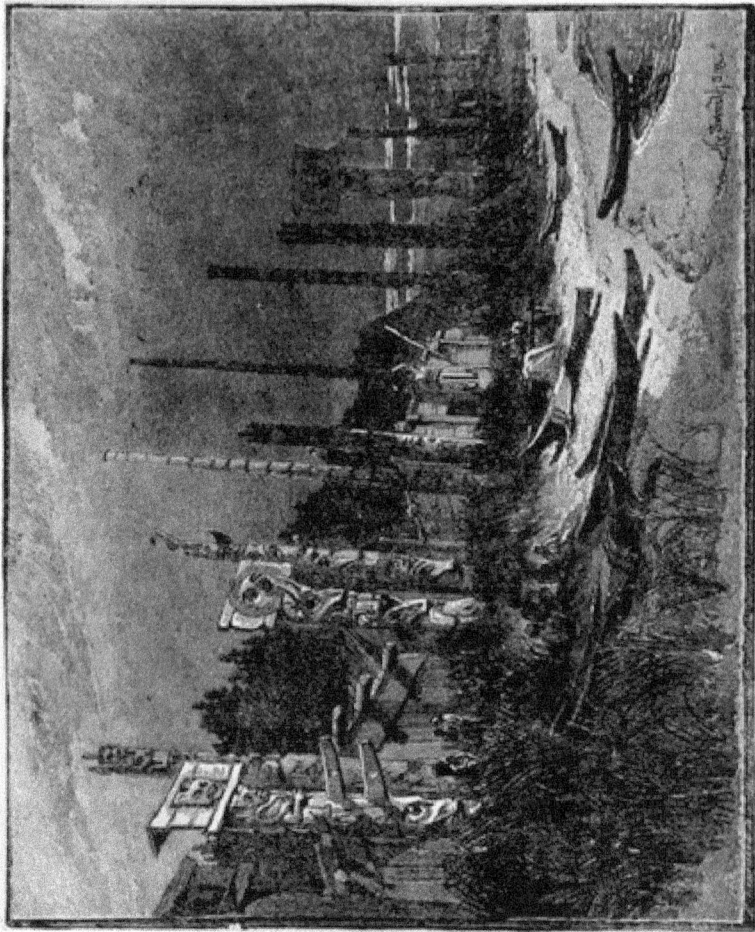

TOTEM POLES.   INDIAN VILLAGE, B.C.

verted Indians, and the squalor and wretchedness of the still pagan Indians on the Reserve near the city. In company with the Rev. Mr. Percival, I visited this village. The house, like most of the Indian lodges on the West Coast, was a large structure of logs with slab roof, occupied in common by several families, but divided into a number of stall-like compartments. Each family had its own fire upon the bare earth floor, and its own domestic outfit. This is very meagre—a few woven mats, a bed upon a raised dais, a few pots and pans. As we entered, a low plaintive croon or wail greeted our ears. This, we found, came from a forlorn-looking woman in wretched garb, crouching beside a few embers. As we drew near she lapsed into sullen silence, from which no effort could move her.

BURIAL.

Yet that these poor people have their tender affections we saw evidence in the neighouring graveyard, in the humble attempts to house and protect the graves of their dead. I noticed one pathetic memorial of parental affection in a little house with a glass window, on which was written the tribute of love and sorrow, " In memory of Jim." Within was a child's carriage, dusty and time-stained, doubtless the baby carriage of Jim. An instinct old as humanity, yet ever new, led the sorrowing parents to devote what was most precious in the memory of their child. Numerous similar evidences of affection were observed in other Indian places of burial.

On this subject the Rev. Dr. McLean, who has large acquaintance as a Methodist missionary with Indian customs, in his charming book, "The Indians of Canada," writes as follows:

"Several modes of burial have been practised by the native tribes. There are several kinds of mounds, descriptive of the customs of the Mound-Builders of

INDIAN GRAVES NEAR VICTORIA, B.C.

pre-historic America. The Tshimpsheans of British Columbia in former years, and the Apaches of to-day, practise cremation. The latter place the body on some sticks of wood, and it is there consumed. Should the person die in a hut it is consumed with all that it contains. Some of the Alaskan Indians embalmed their dead, as the mummies are still to be found in the mummy caves. Some of the native tribes erect scaffolds or place their deceased relatives in the crotches of trees and on the top of some lofty rock. Sometimes an eminence is selected, and again a secluded spot, where a lodge is pitched and the corpse placed within. Graves are also made on the top of the ground and small houses built over them.

"Some tribes killed two young men when a chief died, that their spirits might accompany him by the way. Wrapped in his buffalo robe or blanket the warrior is borne to his grave, generally accompanied by very few of his friends. Beside him, in the lodge, grave or coffin, are placed the relics of the deceased —pipes, tobacco, and many things of greater or less value are deposited there. They believe that everything in nature is possessed of a spirit, and that the spirits of the articles devoted to the deceased depart with him and are used in the spirit world. Thus, when you point to the goods lying at the grave after many days, the natives will tell you that the substance remains, but the spirits live on the spirit of the things. The souls of hatchets and pipes, horses and dogs, go to the "happy hunting ground" for their master's use.

"Upon the death of a chief among the Six Nation Indians, a song of condolence was sung, which " contains the names, laws and customs of their renowned ancestors, and praying to God that their deceased brother might be blessed with happiness in his other state." The Pawnee women, at sunrise and sunset, for three days, go to the graves singing the songs of the dead. Our Plain Indian women cut off their

hair, one of their fingers by the first joint, and make
bloody gashes on their legs.   Sad, indeed, is the wail

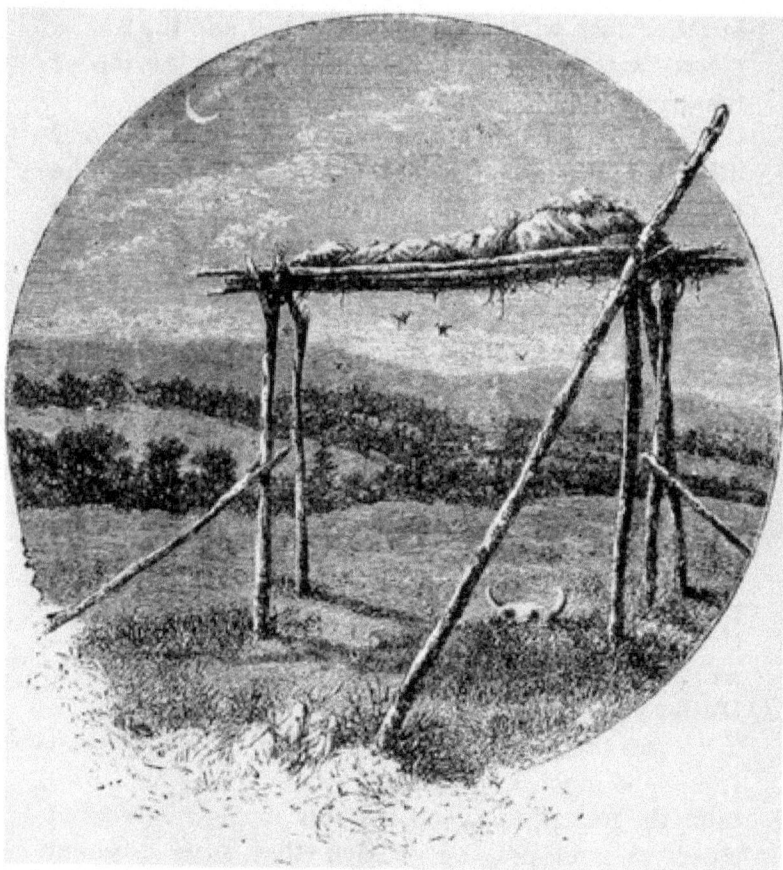

INDIAN GRAVE ON THE PRAIRIES.

of the Indian mothers for the dear ones they have lost.
The native tribes are very much afraid of the dead.
They believe that the spirits go abroad at night and

they are afraid to go out. When passing a grave in the darkness they will run or shout that the spirit may be driven away.

"Indians are strong believers in dreams. They attach a great deal of importance to the visions that pass in review during the silent watches of the night. They impart a reality to the object seen that often-times haunts them on their journeys over mountain and plain. They are afraid of their dead friends, and when they dream that they have seen them, they assert that the spirits of their dead friends have appeared to them.

"While distributing Sunday-school papers among some children, I gave away a copy with an illustration of the raising of Lazarus. On my departure a boy came running after me, stating that the paper was bad, because it had the picture of a ghost on it, and he could not keep it."

SCALPING.

"The Indians," says Dr. McLean, "were always anxious to secure scalps, as the warrior who had the greatest number was held in the highest estimation by the members of his tribe, and feared by his enemies. It was impossible for a warrior to carry the body of his victim to prove his valour to his fellows, so he took the scalp, and showing it to the warriors and people of his tribe, he vaunted his courage and received their applause. The victorious Indian, having thrown his victim, twisted the scalp-lock with his left hand, then cutting the skin around the crown of the head, tore the scalp off. This was done quickly, and then fastening it to his belt, or carrying it in his hand, he hastened to join his comrades or make his escape. After the expedition was over, scalp dances and scalp processions were held. These scalps were worn on days of rejoicing, and at other times hung at their cabin doors. Many scalp-locks have I seen in the years gone by hanging outside the lodges of the Blood Indians, but to-day not a single one is to be seen in all the camp. The scalps and trophies of war were placed on poles, and paraded among the lodges, followed by the warriors, decked in savage finery and hideously painted as for war. We shudder when we read of the cruel warfare and the deeds of blood.

"The reeking scalp and the wild war-whoop seem to belong to savage tribes, and still, during the early years in New England, the colonists and soldiers took the scalps of the Indians, and the officers of justice in America, acting under the British Government, offered large bounties for Indian scalps.

" The first thing to be done, upon the return of a war party having prisoners, was to decide as to the manner of their disposal. The Iroquois generally burned two or three of them, and then distributed the others— men, women and children—among several households for adoption. By this means the Iroquois kept up their strength. When a son or daughter died, the parents engaged a captain to procure someone to fill the place of the deceased. A woman having lost a husband, did in like manner.

"Amongst some of the tribes the prisoners were

subjected to severe torture. They were handed over to
the woman, who mocked and spat upon them, calling
them hard names, and severely taunting and jeering
at them. The brave warrior suffered in silence, or
returned scoff for scoff, urging them to go on with
their cruelty, that he was a man with a brave heart,
and heeded them not. The Blackfeet placed their
prisoners as a mark, and shot at them with their
arrows."

WAMPUM.

A peculiar Indian custom is that of making and
using wampum. "It was made," says Dr. McLean, "in
early times of wood and shells, of various colours, but
similar in size. It was used as a kind of currency
among the tribes, as an ornament of dress, a means of
sending communications, a token of friendship, a record
of historical events, and a pledge at the making of
treaties. The shells, being made into the form of
beads, were perforated, strung on leather thongs, and
used as wampum strings, or woven into belts of various
sizes and designs. The peace belt given to individuals
and tribes, as a token of friendship, was made of white
shells, and the war belts were woven with those of a
dark colour. When a war belt was sent to a tribe
and accepted, it denoted that common cause in war
was to be made by both.

"Wampum strings were given as pay to the per-
formers at the Indian feasts. Among the Iroquois,
wampum strings were employed for narrating historical records. They served as guides to each topic
or subject of address. There was a keeper of these

strings, who thus became the keeper of the Iroquois archives.

"When Peter Jones had his audience with the Queen, he presented a petition and some wampum from the Ojibways of Canada. In speaking of Her Majesty in his journal, he records: 'I then proceeded to give her the meaning of the wampum, and told her that the white wampum signified the loyal and good feeling which prevails amongst the Indians toward Her Majesty and her Government; but that the black wampum was designed to tell Her Majesty that their hearts were troubled on account of their having no title-deeds to their lands; and that they had sent their petition and wampum that Her Majesty might be pleased to take out all the black wampum, so that the string might be all white.'"

Mission Work.

Dr. McLean, who has had himself a successful record as missionary among the Blackfeet, writes as follows:

"Indian missionary work in Canada by Protestants began in earnest with the labours of the Rev. Wm. Case, of the Methodist Church. So deeply was this man of God impressed with his responsibility in carrying to the Indian tribes the word of God, that he travelled almost incessantly, visiting the Indians, urged the missionaries under his care to study the languages, sought out true and well-qualified men to labour, and devised new methods for winning the tribes to Christ. He took several Indian boys and had them sing at missionary meetings in the United States, much to the joy of the people there, and with great profit to the funds of the Church. He organized the Manual Labour School at Alderville, as a training institution for Indian youth. This school became the Indian college, where several of our most successful Indian missionaries were trained. The men directed by Elder Case became the most successful missionaries among the Indians of the Church. His heart was in this work, and, like the sainted John Elliott, the apostle of the Indians, he only ceased to labour for them when his breath ceased.

"As he attended a camp-meeting, he beheld the face of a youth among the converts, who was destined to become one of the most successful Indian missionaries that ever lived. That lad was Kahkewayquonaby—Peter Jones.

"The father of this youth was a white man, who, having loved a modern Pocahontas, married her. Although the lad had spent his childhood in the Indian camps, his father, being a man of education, sent him to school, where he received a fair education. After his conversion, he held prayer meetings among the Indians, taught an Indian school, pursued a course of self-education, and travelled with the missionaries as assistant preacher and interpreter. After his ordination, he became an Indian missionary, with a roving commission. Tribe after tribe, and band after band, he visited; and, as he preached, the power of God fell upon the people, and many were led to rejoice in salvation. On his own mission he went with his Indians into the fields, and taught them how to plough and sow. He encouraged the women to persevere in the study of domestic economy. All day long he would labour in the fields with his people, and, in the evenings, they gathered together in their prayer-meetings. A week or two at home, spent in this manner, and then away he would go on a missionary visit to the tribes scattered throughout the Province of Ontario. He was intensely energetic in his labours for the salvation of men. Such was his influence among the Indians that, when they heard that he was passing through a section of country to attend a meeting at a distant point, the Indians and whites would come for miles to see him, prevail on him to speak a few words to them on religious matters, and, of their own accord, would take up a collection, and, with tears in their eyes, give it to him, as expressive of their love for the Gospel, wishing that they could make it more.

"Twice he appeared before Royalty in England. Everywhere he was preaching to the Indians, or preaching and lecturing in the interests of his work. He did a noble work. Thousands of Indians heard from him the way of life. Many, very many, were led to Christ through his instrumentality. Though he is dead, he is still preaching to the Indians by his Ojibway Hymn Book and New Testament.

"John Sunday—Shawundais—was a Mississauga Indian. Dark and lonely were the early days of his life; but the Gospel reached his heart, and, impelled with love for his fellow-men, he began to tell the

story of God's love to fallen man.   A roving commission was his; for in our forests, and along the rivers
and lakes of Ontario, and farther west, on the shores
of Lake Superior, he sped to declare, in the lonely

JOHN SUNDAY, INDIAN PREACHER.

wigwam and among the scattered bands of red men, the everlasting truth of God. From that day till the present the songs of Zion have been sung, and souls won for Christ by Evans, Rundle, Woolsey, McDougall, and a host of other honest toilers in the mission fields.

"God has blessed with His presence the ministrations of His servants of all the churches in the camps of the Indians of our land.

" A significant fact has been stated as to the value of missionary effort, that it cost the United States Government one million eight hundred and forty-eight thousand dollars to support two thousand two hundred Dakota Indians during seven years of their savage life; but after they were Christianized, it cost only one hundred and twenty thousand dollars to support them during the same length of time.

" In 1840, Robert Terrill Rundle, of the Methodist Church, went to Edmonton and Rocky Mountain House to preach the Gospel to the Cree and Stony Indians. He laboured assiduously for the salvation of these tribes, and rejoiced in seeing many led to Christ. The songs he taught the people in those early days are still remembered by them, and many a heart clings fondly to the memory of those distant years. This faithful man still lives in England, having become superannuated a few years ago. His name will endure in the geography of our western country, for Mount Rundle rears its lofty head in the vicinity of the railroad in the mountains.

"Sinclair, Steinhauer, Woolsey and Brooking laid

the foundation of Christian truth among the Indian tribes in that distant region, supplementing the labours of Evans and Rundle; and from that day thousands of Indians have heard the Gospel news, and rejoiced in its saving power. Many have died in the faith, testifying with their latest breath to the power of Christ to forgive sin.

"The McDougalls, father and son, took up the mantles of the departed missionaries, and the Crees, Stonies and Saulteaux heard anew the story of God's love to man. Song and story around the camp fires were full of spiritual life and joy. The painted savage heard with astonishment the conquests of the Christ, and he acknowledged the Christian Master of Life as his Leader and Friend. Proud hearts were melted as the missionaries sang of Jesus' love and the lodges in the land of the Northern Lights resounded with the shouts of Christian joy.

"Time and space fail in giving to all the faithful toilers among the Crees, Saulteaux and Stonies their meed of praise. Travellers have mentioned their names with reverence, and the Indians treasure the memory of their labours in their hearts. Young, German, Ross, Langford and Semmens are only a few of the self-sacrificing spirits who carried the truth among the lodges, and followed the Indians over the lakes and into the forests, that they might win them for Christ.

"Across the mountains into British Columbia the red men have gone, and there, too, the intrepid spirits have followed them. Duncan, of Metlakahtla, the

English Church missionary, and Thomas Crosby, the
energetic Methodist, have seen many of the Haidas,
Tshimpseans, and other Indian tribes led to forsake
their potlaches and heathen feasts and sacrifices for
the nobler way of the Christian life.   Not content
with preaching to the Indians around Fort Simpson,
and travelling in his canoe, Crosby aroused the missionary spirit in Eastern Canada, which nobly re-
sponded to his call; and the mission yacht, *Glad
Tidings*, was built and equipped, and now is speeding
over the mighty Pacific, carrying the knowledge of
Christ to distant tribes.

"Crosby, Tate, Green, and many others are striving
to plant missions among the tribes along the coast
and in the interior, that they may teach the Indians
how to support themselves honestly and well, and
enjoy the purity and blessedness of the Gospel of
peace.

"Tens of thousands during the past thirty years
have heard with joy the wondrous story of the life
of Christ, and been constrained by its influence to
forsake their customs, and follow the nobler teachings
of the Prince of Peace.

"Only when the final day has come and all the
ransomed have returned to the home of God, shall
the wondrous news be fully told of the races and
tribes of red men who, in simplicity of heart and life,
followed the teachings of the Great Spirit in this
Canada of ours."

POTLACH.

"Among the Indians of the Pacific Coast," says Dr. McLean, "there exists a festival known as 'Potlach.' It is a Chinook word, meaning 'to give,' from the fact that the chief object is to make a distribution of gifts to friends. A chief desiring honour, or an Indian wishing to obtain a good name for himself, will call the people of his own and other tribes to enjoy the abundant provision made for them. Many of the adult members of the tribes will spend years of hard toil, live in poverty, denying themselves the necessaries of life, that they may be able to save a sum sufficient to hold a Potlach.

"At these festivals a single Indian has been known to distribute, in money and various kinds of articles, to the amount of fifteen hundred dollars. At the beginning of the Potlach, the names of the persons to receive the gifts are called aloud, and they come forward in a very indifferent manner to receive a blanket or a gun, but when nearing the end of the distribution there is a general scramble for the property to be given away.

"The Canadian Government has very wisely prohibited these festivals, as they are the cause of retarding the progress of the Indians. The industrious and thrifty alone can hold them, because of their wealth; and the evil becomes a serious one, when such persons will labour for years that they may be honoured with a Potlach. The same thing, in principle at least, is practised among other tribes."

Rev. George McDougall.

The Rev. George McDougall was one of the earnest, most devoted and most successful of the Methodist missionaries in the great North-West—then the Great Lone Land, now becoming the home of thousands of settlers. No man possessed the love and confidence of the native tribes as did he, and through his preaching and teaching hundreds were converted from paganism and became faithful Christians. He may be even said to have become a martyr for the truth, for, in the discharge of his duty, he perished at his post as a missionary of the Cross. The following is a touching account of his death:

The Rev. George McDougall was out on the plains with his son, John, procuring their winter's supply of buffalo meat. They were about thirty miles from home and eight or ten from Fort Bresboise, Bow River. On Monday, 24th January, 1876, in the afternoon, John ran the buffaloes and killed three, and by the time they got them skinned and cut up it was long after dark. They then started for the tent, which was about four miles distant. When they had gone about two miles Mr. McDougall said he would go on to the camp; so saying, he started ahead on horseback and left the sleighs to follow. It was very windy at the time, and the snow drifting in all directions, but the night was not very cold. Sad to say, he wandered far out on the plains, and was lost. John, as soon as he came to the camp and found that his father was not there, commenced firing off

his gun in hopes that his father would hear the report
and come to him; but, alas, he was out of hearing.
When morning arrived John took his horse and

REV. GEORGE M'DOUGALL.

started in search, but the drifting snow had left no
trace.   He searched in all directions until night, when
he came to the conclusion that his father, not being

able to find the camp, had started for home; consequently he came home to see, but when he came into the house there was no father there; so he and his brother David and some others started back in haste, searched again, and found that he had been seen by some half-breeds, who were cutting up buffalo out on the plains, on Tuesday afternoon. We suppose he was snow-blind and could not see. His body was found by a half-breed, who was driving to where he had killed a buffalo, on Saturday, 5th February. When found he looked as though—all hope of life being gone—he had laid down, stretched out, folded his arms, closed his eyes, yielded up the ghost, and the spirit of a dear one had calmly and peacefully passed away from earth to be with God.

A HERO'S EXAMPLE.

The Rev. John Semmens, who knew the sainted George McDougall well, writes the following narrative:

Whether we contemplate his earlier devotion to duty, his patient endeavour in mature manhood, or the sorrows and projects of advancing years, the spectacle is both sublime and inspiring. Few men, since the days of the apostles, have dwelt in more inhospitable places, have enjoyed less of life's comforts, or have seen less direct results of their persistent toil than the hero of this sketch. His was but a voice crying in the wilderness; yet it heralded a living Christ. He was but a John in Patmos; yet he brought to the red man the rich revelation of

God's willingness to save. Like Livingstone in
Africa, having done his best, he lay down to die, with
the fervent prayer on his lips, that God would heal
the "open sore" of the North-West. His facile pen
wrote the most glowing descriptions of the fair and
fertile land which had become his adopted home
His eloquent tongue plead with wondrous importun-
ity for the early occupation of a territory destined to
become of untold importance in the history of
Canada. His fine physical forces were brought into
the most complete employ for the honour of the
Master whom he served. His active mind conceived
plans of campaign, looking out into the future, which
were both wise and far-reaching. His loving heart
embraced in its Christian sympathies Saulteaux and
Crees, Stonies and Blackfeet, Half-breeds and white
men. For these he lived and laboured. His sterling
worth was acknowledged by hunter and trader, by
Government officers and missionaries, by the Church
of God, both at home and abroad. His flag was the
signal of peace among the contending tribes. His
word of honour was as satisfactory as a Magna
Charta.

Arduous and protracted labours at length began
to tell upon a naturally strong constitution. Sore
bereavement left a brave heart sad and weary.
Tardy responses to earnest appeals for reinforcements
weighed heavily upon a hopeful temperament. Yet
he was never known to murmur or complain. His
heart knew and bore its own bitterness. On January
27th, 1876, God released the faithful watchman from

further service. From the loneliness of the Saskatchewan to the friendships of the New Jerusalem, from
the snow-covered plain to the streets paved with
gold, from the cold night air of a sub-Arctic winter
to the genial warmth of the "Summer Land of Song,"
from the weariness of over-taxed energies to the
"Rest that Remaineth," from the freezing body to
the life eternal passed George McDougall at the call
of God :

> " Servant of God, well done !
>   Thy glorious warfare's past ;
>   The battle's fought, the race is won,
>   And thou art crowned at last.

> " Redeemed from earth and pain,
>   Ah ! when shall we ascend,
>   And all in Jesus' presence reign
>   With our translated friend."

His life story is that of a hero and a martyr. George
McDougall was one of the bravest and most devoted
of men. We know of few more touching incidents
than that of the father and son—faint with recent
illness—burying with their own hands their loved
ones in isolation and loneliness, yet caring for and
counselling the hundreds of fever-wasted Indians
around them. The tragic scene of the brave missionary's death is unspeakably pathetic. Such brave
men lay the foundations of empire and of a Christian
civilization—their work is their noblest monument—
being dead, they yet speak.

The late Rev. Enos Langford, who for eight years

was an Indian missionary to the Cree Indians, wrote
the following pathetic poem upon the death of George
McDougall :

> Cold was the night and clear the sky
> While homeward bound, he looked on high
> And saw the star which pointed out
> The place he sought, where sure he thought,
> To rest him for the night.
>
> He spurs his horse, but soon to find
> The heavy trains are left behind ;
> How quickly out of sight and sound !
> Where now is he? we soon shall see
> No traces can be found.
>
> When to the camp his friends draw near—
> " No traces of his footprints here : "
> " What ! where ! can he have missed his way ?
> Haste thee, torch, gun, and faster run."
> " Call from the highest hills !"
>
> In vain they searched, in vain they cried,
> No trace was found, no voice replied ;
> Sad was that night, but sadder still,
> When days had passed, and all at last
> Must count him with the dead.
>
> And is he lost who oft had trod
> Those hills and plains o'er snow and sod ?
> He lost ! who others homeward led !
> Yea, lost is he, though strange it be,
> Who was himself a guide.
>
> Search, search for the remains at least
> Of one so brave, but now at rest ;
>   A hero on the field of strife :
> The Spirit's sword—the written Word,
>   He wielded as for life.

With unrelenting zeal and care,
Some search here and others there ;
    Nor do they stop till they have found—
The place of rest where angels blest—
    His corpse upon the ground.

Him dangers never ceased to yield,
Nor boundaries knew his mission field ;
As kind, as brave, each lingering trace
On George McDougall's smiling face,
Of goodness beaming still.

INDIAN SUN DANCE.

At a meeting of the Canadian Institute of Toronto,
the Rev. Dr. McLean, a Methodist missionary to the
Canadian Indians, gave an account of the barbarous
dances of the Blackfeet Indians. One of the most
interesting is the Sun Dance, which is celebrated every
summer; one of the strangest features of which is
the self-torture of those who are admitted as warriors.
Dr. McLean witnessed one of these ceremonies. A
young man with wreaths of leaves around his head,
ankles and wrists, stepped into the centre of the
lodge. A blanket and pillow were laid upon the
ground, on which he stretched himself. An old man
came and stood over him, and in an earnest speech
told the people of the brave deeds and noble heart of
the young man. After each statement of his virtues
and noble deeds the musicians beat applause.

When the orator ceased, the young man rose, placed
his hands upon the old man's shoulders, and drew
them downwards as a sign of gratitude for the favourable things said about him. He then lay down and

INDIAN BRAVE IN HIS WAR PAINT.

four men held him, while a fifth made incisions or cuts in his breast and back. Two places were marked on each breast, denoting the position and width of each incision This being done, and wooden skewers being in readiness, a double-edged knife was held in the hand, the point touching the flesh. A small piece of wood was placed on the underside to receive the point of the knife when it had gone through, and the flesh was drawn out the desired length for the knife to pierce. A quick pressure and the incision was made, the piece of wood removed, and the skewer inserted from the underside as the knife was being taken out. When the skewer was properly inserted it was beaten down with the palm of the hand of the operator, that it might remain firmly in its place. This being done to each breast, with a single skewer for each, strong enough to tear away the flesh, and long enough to hold the lariats fastened to the top of the sacred pole, a double incision was made on the back of the left shoulder, to the skewer of which was fastened a drum. The young man then rose, and one of the operators fastened the lariats, and the victim went up to the sacred pole, looking exceedingly pale, and threw his arms around it, praying earnestly for strength to pass successfully through the trying ordeal. The prayer ended, he moved backward until the flesh was fully extended, and placing a small bone whistle in his mouth, he blew continuously upon it a series of short sharp sounds, while he threw himself backward and danced until the flesh gave way and he fell. Before tearing himself from the lariats, he seized the drum with both hands, and with a sudden pull tore the flesh on his back, dashing the drum to the ground, amid the applause of the people. The flesh that was hanging was then cut off, and the ceremony was at an end. From two to five persons underwent this torture every Sun Dance. They were afterwards admitted to the band of noble warriors. Frequently it is done in pursuance of a vow to the sun, made in the time of danger and distress.

INDIAN POVERTY AND ITS RELIEF.

Mr. John Semmens writes from Winnipeg, Man., October, 1894, as follows:

Seldom if ever in the history of my missionary work have I witnessed greater poverty than was found last summer at some of the missions in the far north. It always requires more energy than the average Indian gets credit for to keep from hunger and cold in a sub-Arctic wilderness. There are two sources of income possible to him. In the winter months, when the snow lies deep upon the ground, he may hunt for fur, and find a market with the Hudson's Bay Company for all he can bring at fair prices; but when he comes to take up his earnings in tea and sugar, pork and flour, or in blankets, clothing and ammunition, he finds that what appeared to be large earnings are speedily spent, and that the results favourable to himself are meagre and inadequate after all. If it be the right season, he may supplement his wages by the sale of fish ; but here, again, the prices paid are not an inducement, and he soon wearies of the toil which fails to bring with it ample reward. Gradually he has fallen into the habit of drifting with the current of passing time, rousing only when pangs of hunger or stress of weather make inaction impossible, or when the wants of the "mother with the children" appeal with irresistible force to the best instincts of his manhood.

THE BURDEN-BEARER.

The persons of whom we now speak are far beyond the wheat fields of Manitoba, beyond the hire and pay of modern commercial life, beyond the paternal care of the Dominion Government, beyond the annuities and gratuities of the Indian Department. They *work* when they must, *wait* while they can, *want* always.

There were special reasons, however, for the distress of last summer. La grippe had run its disastrous course; measles followed. Many, weakened by the first attack, were unprepared for the second visitation, and fell easy victims to its death-dealing power. Throughout the whole land there was mourning over the dying and the dead.

> " There was no flock, however watched and tended,
>   But one dead lamb was there ;
> There was no fireside, howsoe'er defended,
>   But had one vacant chair."

Many of those who passed away were heads of families, and their children were left to the care of neighbours, who had children of their own to support. What with watching by the sick, grieving over the departed, and caring for the convalescent, not much hunting was done all the long winter through ; and when spring came, the meagre returns of fur did not suffice to prevent abject poverty. Thirteen children in school poorly clad, forty on the hillside in the camps with little or no apparel, one hundred people in church barely presentable, and many more at home who could not go out at all for lack of proper covering. I can assure you it was a great pleasure to us to be able to offer some help in the name of the Christian women of Canada. The boxes sent were just enough to give one to each mission in the district, and while the goods were gladly given and thankfully received, what were they, after all, among so many. Only the most needy received anything at all, and many were hurt to find that they were overlooked in the distribution.

This is a good work, and I trust the godly ladies

associated with you in it will not relax their effort in this direction while the need continues to be so great. We bear our own proportion of the expense of transport, for it costs from one to three dollars per hundred pounds to move freight from this point northward; but we gladly bear our share of the burden, so as to relieve the prevailing distress.

Let it be understood that we do not give indiscriminately.

There are two or three classes who are entitled to receive favours, and these only—widows, orphans, sick persons, and helpless old people—but all who can work are left to care for themselves.

Indian Schools.

On page 113 is a picture of an Indian school in the North-West. The Methodist Church has several such. One of these is at Morley, a place named after Dr. Punshon. Here is the McDougall Orphanage, which commemorates the martyr missionary of the plains, the Rev. George McDougall, who perished from all-night exposure beneath a wintry sky while in the discharge of his duty on his vast mission field. The Indian boys and girls are instructed in reading, writing, the knowledge of the Scriptures, mechanical work, and household duties, by kind and faithful teachers, and thus are fitted to become good citizens and true Christians.

The Rev. A. Langford, a Methodist missionary at Norway House, N.W.T., writes thus of Indian child-life:

The majority of Indian children are allowed to do almost as they please at home. Their parents seldom punish them.

You all know children usually have "tempers of their own," and sometimes when you don't give them what they want, just when they want it, two little hands fly up, and two little feet are set in motion. Well, Indian children act very much like other children. Indeed, if you did not see their black heads and dark faces, I don't see how you could tell—from their actions and voices—whether they were Indian or not, for they seemed to act and cry in English.

Now, these crooked little tempers and naughty dispositions are allowed to develop with the child's growth and years, the parents seldom correcting, but allowing the child to act as it wishes. It reaches manhood like a neglected tree, with many useless branches, which affect its fruitfulness and mar its beauty. These children usually grow up rebellious, sullen, sulky, disobedient and unthankful. However, they do not all display ugly tempers and unpleasant countenances. Many of them are very cheerful, and display considerable wit. But, as a rule, they are hard to manage as servants or companions; for they easily get displeased, and then sulk, and will very likely give you some impudent talk. Those, however, who have had a good training in the mission school are much more reasonable and faithful. There is nothing to prevent them from becoming clever men and women if they had proper training at home. For this reason they do not make successful teachers they do not, or will not, enforce discipline.

Should you ask some of these parents why they do not punish their children for wrong-doing, they will tell you they love them, and if they were to whip them they would always feel sorry for it should the children be taken away from them by death before they grew up. You may think it strange, but children, as a rule, dictate to their parents. In every matter of business they seem to have as much authority as the parents. Often a parent, when in the trading store, will turn to a child of five or six years old and ask what he shall next purchase, or of two articles, which he should take. Thus the parent assumes no responsibility in compelling the child to submit to his wishes or better judgment, and they grow up with the idea that they know all they should know, and whatever they are to learn afterwards is received as news, and not as being necessary information ; hence, in employing them as servants, it is a difficult task to train them without giving offence.

Like some white children, they are soon " too big " to attend either day school or Sunday school ; many of them learn to smoke tobacco ; and once they have killed a deer or trapped some valuable fur, they are men—in their own eyes at least.

We mourn over the ungodly lives of some of our young people on these missions. The parents are to blame in most cases. They refuse to correct them while young, and when they grow up to be men and women, as a rule, do not respect their parents, much less reverence them. "We have had fathers of our

8

INDIAN SCHOOL.

flesh who corrected us, and we gave them reverence."
St. Paul, again, says : "Children, obey your parents
in all things," etc. But, among Indians that precept
appears to be read and observed thus : "Parents, obey
your children in all things."

There are a few exceptions, however, to this rule,
but very few. You will see at once, from what I have
written, the necessity of establishing "Homes,"
"Orphanages," and good day schools, so that these
children may be taught as never will be by their
parents, who were once pagan, and see no necessity for
training and teaching their children. This is not to
be wondered at, for people in other parts of the world
—even in civilized Canada—who have not had the
advantage of good schools, seldom give their children
as liberal an education as they should.

Then, continue the work and pray for these missions,
and schools, and homes, for, be assured, " your labor is
not in vain in the Lord." Had we our choice, we
could willingly leave this work for others, and become
contributors to rather than claimants on the Mission
Fund. While we are here, however, we shall try in
every possible way to enlighten and elevate these
poor people, so as to cheer and encourage you in supporting this glorious cause.

How Indians Treat the Aged.

I had often heard, writes Mr. A. M. Barnes, of
the cruel way in which the Indians treated their old
people, but I could not believe it until I went myself
and saw many of the things of which I now want to
tell you.

The old squaws are made to do all the hard work of the camp, to take the ponies to water, strip up the beef, make the fires, bring the wood, and similar things. When a camp is on the move, they have to carry the tepee poles, rolls of canvas, cooking utensils, and other heavy baggage. When the wood is out they have to go for it, and as these prairies are well-nigh woodless for many miles on a stretch, they have to go a long distance. I have many times seen them passing by our women's school or the parsonage with their backs bent beneath a burden of sufficient weight to load a donkey. They are made to go until they can go no longer; and then, when they grow too old and sick to be of use any more, they are subjected to the most shameful treatment. Even the dogs fare better, for the dogs are well fed, and these miserable old people are not. They are not allowed to eat with the other members of the family, but have to take what is left. Often and often they have only a few crusts and bones thrown to them. The old men are treated as cruelly as the old women, though they get clear of the work even when they are able to do it.

Not long ago some Indians went to the Government agent, and asked him for some old worn-out waggon mules that had been abandoned as of no further use. The agent was about to grant their request, when the thought came to him that he would find out what they wanted with the mules. They hesitated for a while, and wouldn't tell him, but when forced to do so, confessed that they wanted them to kill and feed to their old people. The agent was shocked, and of course did not give them the mules.

All the butchering of the beeves shot down on the plains by the men is done by the women just so long as they are able to do it. When they are not, and are confined to the tepees by sickness and old age, they have been known to crawl forth at night, or in the dusk of the evening, to the spot where the butchering had been done, and to devour the offal that have been scattered about. All this sounds too terrible to be written, but it is true, nevertheless. Many of the old men and women come to the parsonage to beg something to eat from Mrs. Methvin. None of them are ever turned away. The most of them eat like famishing wolves.

Very soon after reaching our mission we went one afternoon to visit some of the tepees. In one of them an old woman was lying. She was perhaps eighty years of age. Her face was shrunken and shrivelled, and her hair almost snow white. It was a bitter cold day. The tepee was full of Indians, and she had been crowded away from the fire. She lay in a corner on a couple of dirty, ragged blankets. She was not only sick, but she was shivering with the cold, for her entire clothing consisted of a thin calico waist and an old skirt. Mr. Methvin knelt beside her, took her hand, and asked her kindly how she was. Oh, how her eyes glowed at the notice he gave her! She sat straight up, and began to talk to him excitedly. Oh, it seemed too good to be true that he had noticed her, a poor, miserable old creature, whom everyone else

scorned, and, even in her hearing, wished out of the
way! My eyes filled with tears. It was a pathetic
scene, but it was by no means the last of the kind I
saw.

Even the little children are taught to scorn and ill-
treat the aged.   They are represented as useless
burdens, and hence ought to be out of the way. Often
the family is so rejoiced to get rid of one of these old
people that the body is hurried to the grave before
the breath has left it.   One of the first things the
teachers at our women's school seek to impress upon
the children when they enter is the keeping of the
fifth commandment.

A young Pottawattamie woman, who is now wedded
to a full-blooded Indian, himself also educated, told
me that a source of the deepest pain to her husband
was the thought of the shameful treatment still
bestowed by his tribe upon old people.

So great is an Indian's contempt for the aged and
infirm that he will never address them direct, but
always looking away from them, and as though
speaking to someone else.   How shocking this must
sound to those who have been taught from their
earliest youth to love and reverence the aged ; and
how it ought to stir them to renewed mission work
in behalf of this savage people, who, when once their
hearts are turned to the gentle promptings of the
Christian religion, are so remorseful of the past and
ready to change their way.

CHRISTIANITY AND THE SIOUX.

In an article giving the results of Christianity among the Sioux Indians, Lieutenant Wassel pays a high tribute to missionaries generally. He writes: " From the sorcery and jugglery of a weazened medicine man he has brought the Sioux to confide in the simple teachings of the Bible. From the barbarous self-immolation of the Sun Dance he has led him to the few rites of Christianity. From the gross sensuality and selfishness of the awful mystery, the Takoo Wakan, manifested and worshipped under the form of gods innumerable, he has built up a faith in one Supreme Being. To-day Episcopalians, Presbyterians and Congregationalists are all well represented in the Dakotas, and have rendered great assistance to the Government in efforts towards civilization. The younger men wear their Y. M. C. A. badges, just as their forefathers wore the dirty medicine charms. The leading men are no longer those who have killed the most Crows or stolen the greatest number of ponies. War songs are replaced by Christian hymns, and ' Jesus Itancan ' now bursts forth from the dusky throats that formerly knew nothing but the murderous ' kte.' The churches and religious societies have certainly quenched the fire of barbarism in the Indian children. Marriage, according to the Christian rites, has succeeded the annual virgin-feast, where a slandered maiden stood face to face with her accuser by the sacred fire, and swore a high-sounding oath to her purity. The disappearance of blanket and breech-

REV. E. R. YOUNG IN INDIAN DRESS.

cloth, long hair and highly-painted faces, is a sign
that the Sioux has succumbed to a stronger civilization, and with his old custom have fallen his old
gods."

MISSION WORK IN THE GREAT NORTH-WEST.

I had received instructions, writes the Rev. E. R.
Young, to visit Oxford Mission, and to do all I
could for its upbuilding.   This mission had had a
good measure of success in years gone by.   A church
and mission-house had been built at Jackson's Bay,
and many of the Indians had been converted.   I left
Norway House in a small canoe, manned by two of
my Christian Indians, one of whom was my interpreter.   With this wonderful little boat I was now to
make my first intimate acquaintance.

For this wild land of broad lakes and rapid rivers
and winding creeks the birch-bark canoe is the boat
of all others most admirably fitted.   It is to the
Indian here what the horse is to his more warlike red
brother on the great prairies, or what the camel is to
those who live and wander amidst Arabian deserts.
The canoe is absolutely essential to these natives in
this land, where there are no other roads than the
intricate, devious water routes.   It is the frailest of
all boats, yet it can be loaded down to the water's
edge, and under the skilful guidance of these Indians,
who are unquestionably the finest canoe men in the
world, it can be made to respond to the sweep of their
paddles, so that it seems almost instinct with life and
reason.   What they can do in it, and with it, appeared
to me at times perfectly marvellous.

Yet, when we remember that for about five months of every year some of the hunters almost live in it, this may not seem so very wonderful. It carries them by day, and in it, or under it, they often sleep by night. At the many portages which have to be made in this land, where the rivers are so full of falls and rapids, one man can easily carry it on his head to the smooth water beyond. In it we have travelled thousands of miles, while going from place to place with the blessed tidings of salvation to these wandering bands scattered over my immense circuit. Down the wild rapids we have rushed for miles together, and then out into great Lake Winnipeg, or other lakes, so far from shore that the distant headlands were scarcely visible. Foam-crested waves have often seemed as though about to overwhelm us, and treacherous gales to swamp us, yet my faithful, well-trained canoe men were always equal to every emergency, and by the accuracy of their judgment, and the quickness of their movements, appeared ever to do exactly the right thing at the right moment. As the result, I came at length to feel as much at home in a canoe as anywhere else, and with God's blessing was permitted to make many long trips to those who could not be reached in any other way, except by dog-trains in winter.

Good canoe-makers are not many, and so really good canoes are always in demand. Frail and light as this Indian craft may be, there is a great deal of skill and ingenuity required in its construction.

Great care is requisite in taking the bark from the tree. A long incision is first made longitudinally in

the trunk of the tree. Then, from this cut, the Indian
begins, and with his keen knife gradually peels off
the whole of the bark, as high up as his incision went,
in one large piece or sheet, as shown in cut on page
126. And even now that he has safely got it off the
tree, the greatest care is necessary in handling it, as
it will split or crack very easily. Cedar is preferred
for the woodwork, and when it can possibly be
obtained, is always used.

Canoes vary in style and size. Each tribe using
them has its own patterns, and it was to me an ever-
interesting sight, to observe how admirably suited to
the character of the lakes and rivers were the canoes
of each tribe or district.

The finest and largest canoes were those formerly
made by the Lake Superior Indians. Living on the
shores of that great inland sea, they required canoes
of great size and strength. These "great north
canoes," as they were called, could easily carry from
a dozen to a score of paddlers, with a cargo of a couple
of tons of goods. In the old days of the rival fur-
traders these great canoes played a very prominent
part. Before steam or even large sailing vessels had
penetrated into those northern lakes, these canoes
were extensively used. Loaded with the rich furs of
those wild forests, they used to come down into the
Ottawa, and thence on down that great stream, often
even as far as to Montreal.

Sir George Simpson, the energetic but despotic
governor of the Hudson's Bay Company for years,
used to travel in one of these birch canoes all the way

TAKING THE BARK FROM THE TREES FOR CANOE-MAKING.

from Montreal up the Ottawa, on through Lake
Nipissing into Georgian Bay ; from thence into Lake
Superior, on to Thunder Bay. From this place, with
indomitable pluck, he pushed on back into the interior,
through the Lake of the Woods, down the tortuous
River Winnipeg into the lake of the same name.
Along the whole length of this lake he annually
travelled, in spite of its treacherous storms and annoy-
ing head winds, to preside over the Council and attend
to the business of the wealthiest fur-trading company
that ever existed, over which he watched with eagle
eye, and in every department of which his distinct
personality was felt.

How rapid the changes which are taking place in
this world of ours! It seems almost incredible, in
these days of mighty steamships going almost everywhere on our great waters, to think that there are
hundreds of people still living who distinctly remember when the annual trips of a great governor were
made from Montreal to Winnipeg in a birch-bark
canoe, manned by Indians.

Of this light Indian craft Longfellow wrote :

> "Give me of your bark, O Birch tree !
> Of your yellow bark, O Birch tree !
> Growing by the rushing river,
> Tall and stately in the valley !
> I a light canoe will build me,
> Build a swift canoe for sailing.
>
> . . . .
>
> "Thus the birch canoe was builded
> In the valley by the river,
> In the bosom of the forest."

We left for Oxford Mission on the 8th of September. The distance is over two hundred miles, through the wildest country imaginable. We did not see a house —with the exception of those built by the beavers— from the time we left our mission-home until we reached our destination. We paddled through a bewildering variety of picturesque lakes, rivers and creeks. When no storms or fierce head-winds impeded us, we were able to make fifty or sixty miles a day. When night overtook us, we camped on the shore. Sometimes it was very pleasant and romantic; at other times, when storms raged and we were drenched with the rain so thoroughly that for days we had not a dry stitch upon us, it was not quite so agreeable.

We generally began our day's journey very early in the morning, if the weather was at all favourable, and paddled on as rapidly as possible, since we knew not when head-winds might arise and stop our progress. The Oxford route is a very diversified one. There are lakes, large and small, across which we had to paddle. In some of them, when the winds were favourable, our Indians improvised a sail out of one of our blankets. Lashing it to a couple of oars, they lifted it up in the favouring wind, and thus very rapidly did we speed on our way.

At times we were in broad beautiful rivers, and then paddling along in little narrow creeks amidst the reeds and rushes. We passed over, or, as they say in that country, "made" nine portages around picturesque falls or rapids. In these portages one of

the Indians carried the canoe on his head. The other
made a great load of the bedding and provisions, all
of which he carried on his back. My load consisted
of the two guns, ammunition, two kettles, the bag
containing my changes of raiment, and a package of
books for the Indians we were to visit. How the
Indians could run so quickly through the portages
was to me a marvel. Often the path was but a narrow ledge of rock against the side of the great granite
cliff; at other times it was through the quaking bog
or treacherous muskeg. To them it seemed to make
no difference. On they went with their heavy loads
at that swinging Indian stride which soon left me
far behind.

To visit the Indians who fish in the waters of
Oxford Lake and hunt upon its shores I once brought
one of our missionary secretaries, the eloquent Rev.
Lachlin Taylor, D.D. We camped for the night on
one of the most picturesque points. The Indians
looked on in amazement while he talked of the beau-
ties of the lake and islands, of the water and the sky.

"Wait a moment, doctor," I said. "I can add to
the wild beauty of the place something that will
please your artistic eye."

I requested two fine-looking Indians to launch one
of the canoes, and to quietly paddle out to the edge
of an island which abruptly rose from the deep, clear
waters before us, the top of which had on it a number
of splendid spruce and balsams, massed together in
natural beauty. I directed the men to drop over the
side of the canoe a long fishing line, and then posing

"REV. LACHLIN TAYLOR, D.D., WAS AN ENTHUSIASTIC FISHERMAN."

them in striking attitudes in harmony with the place,
I asked them to keep perfectly still until every ripple
made by their canoe had died away.

I confess I was entranced by the sight. The reflec-
tions of the canoe and men and of the islands and
rocks were as vivid as the actual realities. It was
one of those sights which come to us but seldom in a
lifetime, where everything is in perfect unison, and
God gives us glimpses of what this world, His foot-
stool, must have been before sin entered.

"Doctor," I said quietly, for my heart was full of
the doxology, "tell me what you think of that vision."

Standing up, with a great rock beneath his feet, in
a voice of suppressed emotion he began. Quietly at
first he spoke, but soon he was carried away with his
own eloquence:

"I know well the lochs of my own beloved Scot-
land, for in many of them I have rowed and fished.
I have visited all the famed lakes of Ireland, and
have rowed on those in the lake counties of England.
I have travelled far and oft on our great American
lakes, and have seen Tahoe, in all its crystal beauty.
I have rowed on the Bosphorus, and travelled in a
felucca on the Nile. I have lingered in the gondola
on the canals of Venice, and have traced Rob Roy's
canoe in the sea of Galilee and on the old historic
Jordon. I have seen, in my wanderings in many
lands, places of rarest beauty, but the equal of this
mine eyes have never gazed upon."

Never after did I see the lake as we saw it that
day.

9

On it we have had to battle against fierce storms, where the angry waves seemed determined to engulf us.   Once, in speeding along as well as we could from island to island, keeping in the lee as much as possible, we ran upon a sharp rock and stove a hole in our canoe.   We had to use our paddles desperately to reach the shore, and when we had done so, we found our canoe half full of water, in which our bedding and food were soaked.   We hurriedly built a fire, melted some pitch, and mended our canoe, and hurried on.

Long years ago a careless, sinful, young Indian rushed into the Mission-house, under the influence of liquor, and threatened to strike me.   But the blessed truth reached his heart, and it was my joy to see him a humble suppliant at the Cross.   His heart's desire was realized.   God has blessedly led him on, and now he is faithfully preaching that same blessed Gospel to his countrymen at Oxford Mission.

In responding to the many Macedonian cries, my circuit kept so enlarging that I had to be "in journey-ings often."   My canoes were sometimes launched in spring, ere the great floating ice-fields had disappeared, and through tortuous open channels we carefully paddled our way, often exposed to great danger.

On one of these early trips we came to a place where, for many miles, the moving ice-fields stretched out before us.   One narrow channel of open water only was before us.   Anxious to get on, we dashed into it, and rapidly paddled ourselves along.   I had two experienced Indians, and so had no fear, but expected some novel adventures—and had them with interest.

Our hopes were that the wind would widen the channel, and thus let us into open water. But, to our disappointment, when we had got along a mile or so in this narrow open space, we found the ice was quietly but surely closing in upon us. As it was from four to six feet thick, and of vast extent, there was power enough in it to crush a good-sized ship; so it seemed that our frail birch-bark canoe would have but a poor chance.

I saw there was a reasonable possibility that when the crash came we could spring on to the floating ice. But what should we do then? was the question, with canoe destroyed and on floating ice far from land.

However, as my Indians kept perfectly cool, I said nothing, but paddled away and watched for the development of events. Nearer and nearer came the ice; soon our channel was not fifty feet wide. Already behind us the floes had met, and we could hear the ice grinding and breaking as the enormous masses met in opposite directions. Now it was only about twenty feet from side to side. Still the men paddled on, and I kept paddling in unison with them. When the ice was so close that we could easily touch it on either side with our paddles, one of the Indians quietly said, "Missionary, will you please give me your paddle?" I quickly handed it to him, when he immediately thrust it with his own into the water, holding down the ends of them so low horizontally under the canoe that the blade end was out of the water on the other side of the boat. The other Indian held his paddle in the same position, although from the other side of the canoe. Almost immediately after the ice crowded in upon us. But as the points of the paddles were higher than the ice, of course they rested upon it for an instant. This was what my cool-headed, clever men wanted. They had a fulcrum for their paddles, and so they pulled carefully on the handle ends of them, and, the canoe sliding up as the ice closed in and met with a crash under us, we found ourselves seated in it on the top of the ice. The craft, although only a frail birch-bark canoe, was not in the least injured.

As we quickly sprang out of our canoe, and carried it away from where the ice had met and was being ground into pieces by the momentum with which it came together, I could not but express my admiration to my man at the clever feat.

On one of my canoe trips, when looking after pagan bands in the remote Nelson River District, I had some singular experiences, and learned some important lessons about the craving of the pagan heart after God.

We had been journeying on for ten or twelve days when one night we camped on the shore of a lake-like river. While my men were busily employed in gathering wood and cooking the supper, I wandered off and ascended to the top of a well-wooded hill which I saw in the distance. Very great, indeed, was my surprise, when I reached the top, to find myself in the presence of the most startling evidences of a degraded paganism.

The hill had once been densely covered with trees, but about every third one had been cut down, and the stumps, which had been left from four to ten feet

INDIAN CONJURER'S MASK.

high, had been carved into rude representations of the human form. Scattered around were the dog-ovens, which were nothing but holes dug in the ground and lined with stones, in which at certain seasons, as part of their religious ceremonies, some of their favourite dogs—white ones were always preferred—were roasted, and then devoured by the excited crowd. Here and there were the tents of the old conjurers and the medicine men, who, combining some knowledge of disease and medicine, with a great deal of superstitious abominations, held despotic sway over the people. The power of these old conjurers over the deluded Indians was very great. They were generally lazy old fellows, but succeeded, nevertheless, in getting the best that was going, as they held other Indians in such terror of their power, that gifts in the shape of fish and game were constantly flowing in upon them. They have the secret art among themselves of concocting some poisons so deadly that a little put in the food of a person who has excited their displeasure will cause death almost as soon as a dose of strychnine. They have other poisons which, while not immediately causing death to the unfortunate victims, yet so affect and disfigure them that, until death releases them, their sufferings are intense and their appearance frightful.

Here on this hill top were all these sad evidences of the degraded condition of the people. I wandered around and examined the idols, the most of which had in front of them, and in some instances on their flat heads, offerings of tobacco, food, red cotton and other things. While there I lingered and mused and prayed, the shadows of the night fell on me, and I was shrouded in gloom. Then the full moon rose up in the east, and, as her silvery beams shone through the trees and lit up these grotesque idols, the scene presented a strange weird appearance. My faithful Indians, becoming alarmed at my long absence—for the country was infested by wild animals—were on the search for me when I returned to the camp fire. We ate our evening meal, sang a hymn, and bowed in prayer. Then we wrapped ourselves up in our blankets, and lay down on the granite rocks to rest. Although our bed was hard and there was no roof above us, we slept sweetly, for the day had been one of hard work and strange adventure.

After paddling about forty miles the next day we reached the Indians of that section of the country, and remained several weeks among them. We held three religious services every day, and between these services taught the people to read in the syllabic characters. They listened attentively, and the Holy Spirit applied these truths to their hearts and consciences so effectively that they gladly received them. A few more visits effectually settled them in the truth. They have cut down their idols, filled up the dog-ovens, torn away the conjurer's tents, cleared the forest, aud banished every vestage of the old life. And there, at what is called the "Meeting of the Three Rivers," on that very spot where idols were worshipped amidst horrid orgies, and where the yells, rattles and drums of the old conjurers and medicine men were heard continuously for days and nights, there is now a little church, where these same Indians, transformed by the glorious Gospel of the Son of God, are "clothed and in their right mind, sitting at the feet of Jesus."

My visits to Nelson River so impressed me with the fact of the necessity of some zealous missionary going down there and living among the people, that, in response to appeals made, the Rev. John Semmens, whose heart God had filled with missionary zeal, and who had come out to assist me at Norway House, nobly resolved to undertake the work. He was most admirably fitted for the arduous and responsible task ; but no language of mine can describe what he had to suffer. His record is on high. The Master has it all, and He will reward. Great were his successes and signal his triumphs.

At that place, where I found the stumps carved into idols, which Brother Semmens has so graphically described, the church, mainly through his instrumentality and personal efforts, has been erected. In the last letter which I have received from that land the writer says: " The Indians now all profess themselves to be Christians. Scores of them by their lives and testimonies assure us of the blessed consciousness that the Lord Jesus is indeed their own loving Saviour. Every conjurer's drum has ceased ; all vestiges of the old heathenish life are gone, we believe, forever."

"The wilderness and the solitary place shall be glad for them, and the desert shall rejoice and blossom as the rose."

Grandly has this prophecy been fulfilled, and dwarfs into insignificance all the sufferings and hardships endured in the pioneer work which I had in begin-

"WITH HIS LIGHT CANOE HE CAN GO
ALMOST ANYWHERE."

ning this Mission. With a glad heart I rejoice that
"unto me, who am less than the least of all saints, is
this grace given, that I should preach among the
Gentiles the unsearchable riches of Christ."

THE SONG OF HIAWATHA.

Longfellow's beautiful Song of Hiawatha recounts
many of the legends and traditions of the red man of
the forest. We quote a few passages.

> Ye, whose hearts are fresh and simple,
> Who have faith in God and Nature,
> Who believe, that in all ages
> Every human heart is human,
> That in even savage bosoms
> There are longings, yearnings, strivings,
> For the good they comprehend not,
> That the feeble hands and helpless,
> Groping blindly in the darkness,
> Touch God's right hand in that darkness
> And are lifted up and strengthened :—
> Listen to this simple story,
> To this Song of Hiawatha !
> Ye, who sometimes in your rambles
> Through the green lanes of the country,
> Where the tangled barberry-bushes
> Hang their tufts of crimson berries
> Over stone walls grey with mosses,
> Pause by some neglected graveyard,
> For a while to muse, and ponder
> On a half-effaced inscription,
> Written with little skill of song-craft,
> Homely phrases, but each letter
> Full of hope, and yet of heart-break,

Full of all the tender pathos
Of the Here and the Hereafter :—
Stay and read this rude inscription,
Read this Song of Hiawatha !

PICTURE WRITING.

" In those days," said Hiawatha,
" Lo ! how all things fade and perish !
From the memory of the old men
Fade away the great traditions.

" Great men die and are forgotten,
Wise men speak ; their words of wisdom
Perish in the ears that hear them,
Do not reach the generations
That, as yet unborn, are waiting
In the great, mysterious darkness
Of the speechless days that shall be !

" On the grave-posts of our fathers
Are no signs, no figures painted ;
Who are in those graves we know not,
Only know they are our fathers.
Of what kith they are and kindred,
From that old, ancestral Totem,
Be it Eagle, Bear, or Beaver
They descended, this we know not,
Only know they are our fathers.

" Face to face we speak together,
But we cannot speak when absent,
Cannot send our voices from us
To the friends that dwell afar of."
Thus, said Hiawatha, walking
In the solitary forest,
Pondering, musing in the forest,
On the welfare of his people,

From his pouch he took his colours,
Took his paints of different colours,
On the smooth bark of a birch tree

Painted many shapes and figures—
Wonderful and mystic figures—
And each figure had a meaning,
Each some word or thought suggested.

Life and Death he drew as circles,
Life was white, but Death was darkness ;
Sun and moon and stars he painted,
Man and beast, and fish and reptile,
Forests, mountains, lakes, and rivers.

For the earth he drew a straight line,
For the sky a bow above it ;
White the space between for day-time,
Filled with little stars for night-time ;
On the left a point for sunrise,
On the right a point for sunset,
On the top a point for noon-tide,
And for rain and cloudy weather
Waving lines descending from it.

Footprints pointing towards a wigwam
Were a sign of invitation,
Were a sign of guests assembling ;
Bloody hands with palms uplifted
Were a symbol of destruction,
Were a hostile sign and symbol.

All these things did Hiawatha
Show unto his wondering people,
And interpret their meaning,
And he said : " Behold, your grave-posts
Have no mark, no sign, no symbol.
Go and paint them all with figures,
Each one with his household symbol,
With its own ancestral Totem ;
So that those who follow after
May distinguish them and know them."

And they painted on the grave-posts
Of the graves yet unforgotten,
Each his own ancestral Totem,

Each the symbol of his household—
Figures of the Bear and Reindeer,
Of the turtle. Crane, and Beaver,
Each inverted as a token
That the owner was departed,
That the chief who bore the symbol
Lay beneath in dust and ashes.

Thus it was that Hiawatha,
In his wisdom, taught the people
All the mysteries of painting,
All the art of Picture-Writing,
On the smooth bark of the birch tree,
On the white skin of the reindeer,
On the grave-posts of the village.

WINTER AND FAMINE.

Now, o'er all the dreary Northland,
Mighty Peboan, the Winter,
Breathing on the lakes and rivers,
Into stone had changed their waters.
From his hair he shook the snow-flakes,
Till the plains were strewn with whiteness,
One uninterrupted level,
As if, stooping, the Creator
With His hand had smoothed them over.
O the long and dreary Winter !
O the cold and cruel Winter !
Ever thicker, thicker, thicker
Froze the ice on lake and river,
Ever deeper, deeper, deeper
Fell the snow o'er all the landscape,
Fell the covering snow, and drifted
Through the forest, round the village.

Hardly from his buried wigwam
Could the hunter force a passage ;
With his mittens and his snow-shoes
Vainly walked he through the forest,

Sought for bird or beast and found none,
Saw no track of deer or rabbit,
In the snow beheld no footprints,
In the ghastly, gleaming forest,
Fell, and could not rise from weakness,
Perished there from cold and hunger.
   O the Famine and the Fever !
O the wasting of the famine !
O the blasting of the fever !
O the wailing of the children !
O the anguish of the women !
   All the earth was sick and famished,
Hungry was the air around them,
Hungry was the sky above them,
And the hungry stars in heaven
Like the eyes of wolves glared at them !
   Forth into the empty forest
Rushed the maddened Hiawatha ;
In his heart was deadly sorrow,
In his face a stony firmness ;
On his brow the sweat of anguish
Started, but it froze, and fell not.
Into the vast and vacant forest
On his snow-shoes strode he forward.
   "Gitche Manito the Mighty !'
Cried he with his face uplifted
In that bitter hour of anguish,
"Give your children food, O father !
Give us food, or we must perish !
Give me food for Minnehaha,
For my dying Minnehaha !"

DEATH OF MINNEHAHA.

   In the wigwam with Nokomis,
With those gloomy guests that watched her,
With the Famine and the Fever,
She was lying, the Beloved,

She the dying Minnehaha.
" Look ! " she said, " I see my father
Standing lonely at his doorway,
Beckoning to me from the wigwam,
In the land of the Dacotahs ! "
" No, my child ! " said old Nokomis,
" 'Tis the smoke that waves and beckons ! "
" Ah ! " she said, " the eyes of Pauguk
Glare upon me in the darkness ;
I can feel his icy fingers
Clasping mine amid the darkness :
Hiawatha ! Hiawatha ! "

Over snow-fields waste and pathless,
Under snow-encumbered branches,
Homeward hurried Hiawatha,
Empty-handed, heavy-hearted,
Heard Nokomis moaning, wailing,
" Would that I had perished for you,
Would that I were dead as you are ! "
And he rushed into the wigwam,
Saw the old Nokomis, slowly
Rocking to and fro and moaning,
Saw his lovely Minnehaha
Lying dead and cold before him ;
And his bursting heart within him
Uttered such a cry of anguish,
That the forest moaned and shuddered,
That the very stars in heaven
Shook and trembled with his anguish.

Then they buried Minnehaha ;
In the snow a grave they made her,
In the forest deep and darksome,
Underneath the moaning hemlock ;
Clothed her in her richest garments,
Wrapped her in her robes of ermine,
Covered her with snow, like ermine ;
Thus they buried Minnehaha.

And at night a fire was lighted,
On her grave four times was kindled,
For her soul upon its journey
To the Islands of the Blessed.
From his doorway Hiawatha
Saw it burning in the forest,
Lighting up the gloomy hemlock ;
From his sleepless bed uprising,
Stood and watched it at the doorway,
That it might not be extinguished,
Might not leave her in the darkness.
    " Farewell !" said he, " Minnehaha,
Farewell, O my Laughing Water !
All my heart is buried with you,
All my thoughts go onward with you !
Came not back again to labour,
Come not back again to suffer,
Where the Famine and the Fever
Wear the heart and waste the body.
Soon my task will be completed,
Soon your footsteps I shall follow
To the Islands of the Blessed,
To the kingdom of Ponemah :
To the Land of the Hereafter ! "

THE PROPHECY.

    " O my children ! my poor children !
Listen to the words of wisdom,
Listen to the words of warning.
From the lips of the Great Spirit,
From the Master of Life who made you !
    " I have given you lands to hunt in,
I have given you streams to fish in.
I have given you bear and bison,
I have given you roe and reindeer,
I have given you brant and beaver,

Filled the marshes full of wild-fowl,
Filled the rivers full of fishes ;
Why then are you not contented ?
Why then will you hunt each other ?

"I am weary of your quarrels,
Weary of your wars and bloodshed,
Weary of your prayers for vengeance,
Of your wranglings and dissensions ;
All your strength is in your union,
All your danger is in discord ;
Therefore be at peace henceforward,
And as brothers live together.

"I will send a Prophet to you,
A Deliver of the nations,
Who shall guide you and shall teach you,
Who shall toil and suffer with you.
If you listen to his counsels,
You shall multiply and prosper ;

If his warnings pass unheeded,
You will fade away and perish !"

THE MISSIONARY.

From the distant land of Wabun,
From the farthest realms of morning
Came the Black-Robe chief, the Prophet.
He the Priest of Prayer, the Pale-face,
With his guides and his companions.

And the noble Hiawatha,
With his hands aloft extended,
Held aloft in sign of welcome,
Waited, full of exultation,
Till the birch canoe with paddles
Grated on the shining pebbles.
Stranded on the sandy margin,
Till the Black-Robe chief, the Pale-face,
With the cross upon his bosom,
Landed on the sandy margin.

10

Then the joyous Hiawatha
Cried aloud and spake in this wise :
"Beautiful is the sun, O strangers,
When you come so far to see us !
All our town in peace awaits you,
All our doors stand open for you ;
You shall enter all our wigwams,
For the heart's right hand we give you."
    And the Black-Robe chief made answer,
Stammered in his speech a little,
Speaking words yet unfamiliar :
"Peace be with you, Hiawatha,
Peace be with you and your people,
Peace of prayer, and peace of pardon,
Peace of Christ, and joy of Mary !"
    Then the Black-Robe chief, the Prophet,
Told his message to the people,
Told the purport of his mission,
Told them of the Virgin Mary,
And her blessed Son, the Saviour ;
How in distant lands and ages
He had lived on earth as we do ;
How he fasted, prayed, and laboured ;
How the Jews, the tribe accursed,
Mocked Him, scourged Him, crucified Him ;
How He rose from where they laid Him,
Walked again with His disciples,
And ascended into heaven.
    And the chiefs made answer, saying :
"We have listened to your message,
We have heard your words of wisdom.
We will think on what you tell us.
It is well for us, O brothers,
That you come so far to see us !"
    Then they rose up and departed
Each one homeward to his wigwam,

To the young men and the women,
Told the story of the strangers
Whom the Master of Life had sent them
From the shining land of Wabun.
   From his place rose Hiawatha,
Bade farewell to old Nokomis,
Bade farewell to all the young men,
Spake persuading, spake in this wise ·
   " I am going, O my people,
Listen to their words of wisdom,
Listen to the truth they tell you,
For the Master of Life has sent them
From the land of light and morning ! "

METHODIST MISSIONS IN LABRADOR.

Not only among the Indians, but among the Eskimo, has our Church faithful missionaries. Of the latter the Rev. H. C. Hatcher, B.D., thus writes:

The long Labrador winter is past, the snow is over, but not all gone ; the time of the singing of birds is come, and the voices of our hardy fishermen are beginning to be heard on the coast.

The winter was unusually severe, and ice formed early. Snow also came in abundance, and with the hard frosts travelling was beautiful after Christmas. Our mode of travelling here in the winter is somewhat the same as that of our brethren in the North-West. We have a comatick made of wood, about seven feet by two, the runners of which are shod with iron, or whalebone. On this we place our luggage, and ride ourselves. To this comatick, made fast by rope or deer-skin traces, we have from six to a dozen dogs, who sometimes dash along at an incredible speed. Sometimes it is over the ponds or along valleys we go. At other times it is over hill and dale, when we often have to be very careful how we descend the hills. The steeper the descent the better pleased seem to be the dogs, and consequently the faster they go. Many a time, in spite of holding on hard, have I found myself landed serenely among the snow-drifts, or rolling down hill, and have been glad to quickly join dogs, and perhaps driver, some

ESKIMO COMATICK.

little distance on. By two simple words, "La," and "Rutter," the driver can turn the head dog to the right or left; the other dogs, of course, play "follow the leader." Thus, in winter time, besides on snow-shoes, we visit the outlying settlements and preach the glorious Gospel of the blessed God.

At Red Bay, in the month of November, we were blessed with some manifestations of the divine favour. God's people were quickened, and about a dozen penitents were found anxiously inquiring, "What must I do to be saved?" Half of these since have

been admitted as members of the Church, while
others are still in classes on trial. It was a "season
of grace and sweet delight" long to be remembered.
We pray that in every place on this ice-bound coast
the melting fire of Jesus' love may be felt.

Death, as usual, was busy among us, smiting down
our members. One white sister was drowned through
a hole in the ice. But a few hours before I met the

ESKIMO SEAL-SKIN TENTS.

class of which she was a member, when she testified
of her love for the Redeeemer, and heartily joined
with us in singing part of that glorious hymn com-
mencing, "O Thou, to whose all-searching sight." At
my request she had also, with another sister, engaged
in prayer at the close of the meeting. As I was
called up in the night for advice (for here the minister
must be doctor as well as everything else), I thought,

as I felt the lifeless hands and gazed on the pallid
face, what need there was to be always ready, and
how good it was for me, as her pastor, to be able to
say :

> " Go, by angel guards attended,
> To the sight of Jesus, go ! "

Shortly before Christmas I was called to visit
another woman, at a distance, who was in a dying
state. As I prescribed, seemingly in vain, for body
and soul, I felt how terribly sad yet sorrowfully true
these words were :

> " Oh, dark ! dark ! dark ! I still must say,
> Amid the blaze of Gospel day."

Such are the contrasts in the experience of the
Methodist missionary. What need for thanksgiving
to God, by those who have had many privileges and
are saved. Yes, and what need to let the lamp of
truth be sent everywhere " to give light and to save
life." Thank God, the Church begins to shake itself
from the dust and to arise to duty.

THE MISSION BOAT "EVANGELIST."

No doubt many of those who so nobly collected
for a mission boat for Labrador will be glad to know
that she has been of great service to the missionary.
By its help I was enabled to visit many places to
the north and west of Red Bay, and preach "the
unsearchable riches of Christ." She is rightly named
the *Evangelist*, as she was given for evangelistic

purposes. When I think of the thousands of souls along the coast for the fishing season, who need the Bread of Life, I ask, What is one among so many? or, in the words of the apostle, "Who is sufficient for these things?" Nevertheless we labour and pray, "Thy kingdom come."

A few vessels have arrived. One put in here last Saturday with death on board. Tuesday another came with death there also, the person being a poor woman who had passed away two days before. She was a child of God; and, according to the testimony of those who journeyed with her, she affectionately bade her children and husband farewell, testifying her happiness in Christ, and when speech failed her, waved her hand in holy triumph. All this amid the rocking of the vessel. Thank God, the religion of Jesus fits for death and makes a downy pillow anywhere. Yesterday we laid her in the place for non-residents in our graveyard, in sure and certain hope of the resurrection to eternal life. They told me one of her dying utterances was, "Tell Mr. Hatcher I am going to be with Jesus."

Thus our hardy fisher-folk come from their homes and sanctuaries in Newfoundland and elsewhere to this coast, and your missionary strives to "point to the all-atoning blood" and cry, "God so loved the world." Oh, for more men and means! Some Sunday-school papers were sent me last year, and I was enabled thus to scatter now and then a *Sunbeam* and a few *Pleasant Hours.*

" Ready the fields before us lie,
 For harvest ripe and white :
We hail the dawn which heralds day,
 Passed is the long dark night,
The labourer's hand will gather sheaves—
 Increasing, more and more,
In souls washed whiter than the snows
 Of frozen Labrador."

Mission Life in the Far North.

The Rev. John MacDougall thus recounts some of his missionary experiences:

An early start, with slow but steady driving, for the roads are heavy, and we continue our journey to Whitefish Lake. Every turn of the road is instinct with memories of the days that are gone.

Yonder I camped alone one winter's night, no blankets, no food, but a rousing toothache, which kept me awake and doubtless also kept me from freezing. Over there I once ran down a hill and across a valley and up another hill, perhaps faster than a man ever did. First, because I was naturally swift of foot; second, because the whole of a big buffalo bull was after me. Head down, tail up, on he came. What signified two feet of snow ! I flew and did not waste any energy looking behind until I reached the top of the next hill. I can laugh now as I see myself touching the snow-covered prairie here and there, and by leaps and bounds fleeing from the huge " King of the Plains." We killed him and packed part of the meat portions of his carcase on our dog-sleds, and notwithstanding we left all the head and neck and back and

rump bones, yet the meat we took home weighed 960 pounds. No wonder I went as one inspired, and undoubtedly I was for the time.

Here is the hill where I had good Brother Wolsey buried under his overturned cariole, in the snow, while I put the "fear of death" in his dogs, who, before that, had looked back at me when I called to them instead of bounding on as they should have done, the lazy brutes knowing full well that Mr. Wolsey, wrapped in robes and tucked into the coffin-like cariole, was helpless, and that I, away behind my own dogs, with the narrow track and the very deep snow between us, could not get at them when I would. But, when my old friend upset and rolled over and over to the foot of the hill, and there remained, both cariole and man upside down; why, then my chance came, and I went for those dogs in a way that made them jump when I spoke to them after that.

THE HUDSON'S BAY COMPANY.

In the year 1670, at the solicitation of Prince Rupert and the Duke of Albemarle, King Charles II. created by Royal Charter the "Company of Merchant Adventurers trading to Hudson's Bay." With characteristic lavishness the King granted to this company the sole trade and commerce of the vast and vaguely-defined regions to which access may be had through Hudson's Straits. Forty years before this, Louis XIII. had made a similar grant to the "Company of New France," and, for nearly a hundred years, there was a keen and eager rivalry between these hostile corporations. In order to control the lucrative fur-trade, the Hudson's Bay Company planted forts and factories at the mouths of the Moose, Albany, Nelson, Churchill, and other rivers flowing into Hudson's Bay. Again and again, adventurous bands of Frenchmen, like D'Iberville and his companions, made bloody raids upon these posts, murdering their occupants, burning the stockades, and carrying off the rich stores of peltries.

Growing bolder with success, the French penetrated the vast interior as far as the head-waters of the Mississippi, the Missouri and the Saskatchewan, and reached the Rocky Mountains long before any other white man had visited these regions. They planted trading-posts and small palisaded forts at important river junctions and on far-off lonely lakes, and wrote their names all over this great continent, in the designation of cape and lake and stream, and other great features of nature. The *voyageurs* and *coureurs de bois*, to whom this wild, adventurous life was full of fascination, roamed through the forests and navigated the countless arrowy streams, and Montreal and Quebec snatched much of the spoil of this profitable trade from the hands of the English company. Every little far-off trading-post and stockaded fort felt the reverberations of the English guns which won the victory of the Plains of Abraham, whereby the sovereignty of those vast regions passed away forever from the possession of France.

After the conquest, numerous independent fur-traders engaged in this profitable traffic. In 1783

A FORT OF THE HUDSON'S BAY COMPANY IN THE OLDEN TIME.

these formed a junction of interests and organized the North-West Company. For forty years this was one of the strongest combinations in Canada. Its energetic agents explored the vast North-West regions. Sir Alexander Mackenzie, in 1789, traced the great river which bears his name, and first reached the North Pacific across the Rocky Mountains. In 1808, Simon Frazer descended the gold-bearing stream which perpetuates his memory; and, shortly after, Thompson explored and named another branch of the same great river.

Keen was the rivalry with the old Hudson's Bay Company, and long and bitter was the feud between the two great corporations, each of which coveted a broad continent as a hunting-ground and preserve for game.

In the early years of the present century the feud between the rival companies was at its height. With the skill of an experienced general, Thomas Douglas, Earl of Selkirk, then Governor of the Hudson's Bay Company, resolved to establish a colony of his countrymen at the junction of the Red River with the Assiniboine, the key of the mid-continent.

In the year 1812 the first brigade of colonists reached Red River by way of Hudson's Bay. A stern welcome awaited them. Hardly had they arrived at the site of the proposed settlement when an armed band of Nor'-Westers, plumed and painted in Indian fashion, appeared and commanded the colonists to depart. They were compelled to submit, and took refuge at the Hudson's Bay post at Pembina. Undaunted by this failure, they returned in the spring, built log-houses and planted their wheat. Again they were driven away and their homes burnt. With dogged perseverance they returned, and after eight years of failures the first harvest was reaped. The colony now struck its roots deep into the soil and

INDIAN HALF-BREED AND DOG.

flourished year by year, and by 1868 had increased to a population of about 12,000.

After forty years of rivalry, in 1821 the Hudson's Bay and North-West companies combined their forces, and were confirmed by the Imperial Parliament in the monopoly of trade through the wide region stretching from Labrador to the Pacific Ocean. The government of the united company, while jealously exclusive of rival influence, was patriarchal in character, and through the exclusion, for the most part, of intoxicating liquors, greatly promoted the welfare of the Indians and repressed disorder throughout its wide domains.

In 1868, the Rupert's Land Act was passed by the British Parliament, and, under its provisions, the Hudson's Bay Company surrendered to the Crown its territorial rights over the vast region under its control. The conditions of this surrender were as follows: The Company was to receive the sum of £300,000 sterling in money, and grants of lands around its trading-posts to the extent of fifty thousand acres in all. In addition, it is to receive, as it is surveyed and laid out in townships, one-twentieth of all the land in the great fertile belt south of the Saskatchewan.

In April, 1869, the Dominion Government passed an Act, providing for the temporary government of the entire region, under the designation of the North-West Territory. Surveying parties were sent into the Red River country for the purpose of laying out roads and townships. This somewhat alarmed the people, lest this movement should in some way prejudice their title to their land.

Jealousies were awakened among the settlers, and fanned into armed rebellion by unscrupulous agitators. In 1870, Colonel Garnet Wolseley led a force of 1,200 men, regulars and militia from Ontario and Quebec, through the then wilderness to Fort Garry. The conspirators fled ; the loyal inhabitants joyfully acknowledged the Queen's authority. The Dominion Government took possession of this vast territory and divided it into the Province of Manitoba and several territories, each with their own Local Government. In the land where they for so long held regal sway the Hudson's Bay Company are now merely traders and store-keepers.

In 1868 the Rev. George Young, D.D., was sent to Fort Garry to establish a Methodist mission at that important place. Through his consecrated zeal and judicious labours Methodism was firmly planted in that country. During the troublous times of the Riel Rebellion, Dr. Young was a tower of strength to the infant cause of Methodism. It is largely through his labours and those of his faithful successors, that in the Manitoba and North-West Conference there are to-day 155 ministers, 512 congregations, 12,500 Sunday-school scholars, 70 Epworth Leagues, and over 15,000 Church members.

PAKAN, THE INDIAN CHIEF.

Among the Christian Indians of the far north land, writes the Rev. E. R. Young, the Sabbath is most faithfully observed. All hunting and fishing ceases, and the people quietly and reverently keep holy the day of rest. Long and patiently did the missionaries have to toil, and much was the opposition they had to encounter ere success crowned their efforts and this pleasing state of affairs was reached.

The following incident will give some idea of the

REV. GEORGE YOUNG, D.D.

difficulties in the way of their living up to the prin-
ciples of the Gospel they have now accepted, and the
sturdy character and boldness they frequently mani-
fest. Their personal comfort or interest is not for a
moment thought of when conscience is at stake, and
hunger will be patiently endured rather than that their
convictions of duty should be sacrificed.

Pakan is the name of the honoured chief of the
Indians at White Fish and Saddle Lake. He is the
worthy successor of the noble Maskepetoon, the chief
who, on hearing a sermon from the prayer of the Lord
Jesus for his murderers, showed his sincere desire to
become a Christian by forgiving the murderer of his
own son.

These Indians, of whom Pakan is now the chief,
years ago made a treaty with the Dominion Government of Canada, in which they ceded away their
rights to a vast area of fertile land, which is now
rapidly filling up with white settlers. In return for
this the Government agreed to give to these Indians
annually a certain sum of money and a large quantity
of supplies.

Not very long ago the Government Commissioner,
who was paying the treaty money to the different
tribes in the West, sent word to Pakan and his people
that on a certain date he would meet them at a
designated place, for the purpose of paying them their
money and distributing among them their annual
supplies.

The Indians were promptly on hand at the appointed
place, although some of them had to come long dis-

tances from their homes or hunting-grounds. Owing
to the assurance of the Commissioner that he would,
without fail, be on hand with the supplies on the date
mentioned, the Indians carried with them only food
sufficient to last them and their families up to the date
of the gathering.

To their discomfort, they found that although the
abundant supplies of food were on hand, yet the Commissioner had not arrived to distribute them. Several
days passed by, and still he failed to appear.

Very naturally the people became hungry, and
yet their sense of honesty and honour were such that,
although they well knew that the supplies in their
midst, unguarded and in their power, really belonged
to them, yet they patiently endured the pangs of
hunger day after day, while earnestly looking for the
arrival of the big man and his attendants to distribute
the food.

Human nature has its limits, and so, after some
days of absolute fasting, a few of the more restive ones
began to think it was about time they quieted the
cries of their hungry families by helping themselves
to these supplies, now that the Commissioner had so
broken his word to them by failing to appear.

When Pakan heard these muttering, he said, in
language not to be misunderstood : "No ; we will not
touch these things. We have not broken a law of the
Government since we made the treaty, and although
we are hungry, we will not begin now." Then he
added: "But this will I do. As we are suffering for our
supplies, I will ride until I meet that white man, and
tell him of our hungry condition because of his delay."

Suiting the action to his words, for Pakan is a man
of prompt action when his mind is once made up, he
was soon mounted on a fleet horse, and, accompanied
by one attendant, was in a few minutes galloping over
the prairies in the direction he was confident the Commissioner would come. Very correct was he in his
surmisings; for after a rapid ride of not more than
ten miles, he found the big man and his party, who,
leisurely travelling along, had that evening already
pitched their tents for the night.

Riding into his camp, Pakan roused him up, and
said: "I thought you would be camped here. My
men are hungry, for they have waited long. They
wanted to help themselves, but I said, 'No, wait until
I see the paymaster.' Now, I have found you, and I
want you to send a man back with me to divide the
food among my hungry people."

"Oh," said the paymaster, "those provisions are all
yours, so just wait here with us until to-morrow
morning, and then we will all ride on to your camp,
and then we will at once divide the supplies among
your people."

"But to-morrow is Sunday," said the brave Christian
chief.

"Well," replied the white man, "my religion is not
so strict but I can give you out your provisions on
that day."

Pakan's reply is worth remembering. He said:
"I do not know what your religion teaches, but this
I do know, that our religion teaches us to provide for
the Lord's Day on Saturday; and so, if you will not

give us the provisions to-night, we will not take them
on the morrow, hungry though we are."

" Why," replied the paymaster, " I thought we would
camp here this Saturday night, and then, going on
early to your camp to-morrow, would at once distribute the supplies ; and then, later on in the day,
have our annual Council talk, and then we would be
ready to pay the treaty money on Monday."

The reply of the noble chief to this was short, but
emphatic : " If we will not take food, we certainly
will not have the talk on the Sunday."

From this position the chief would not move. The
result was, the dilatory paymaster was obliged to
order one of his subordinate officials to return that
Saturday night, through the darkness, with Pakan,
and see to the distribution of the food among the
people.

The next day the big white man made his entry in
the camp of Pakan. No salute of firearms or demon-
strative greeting welcomed him. In that large en-
campment there was nothing but the quiet decorum
of a restful Sabbath day. Vainly did the big official
try to gather the Indians in Council for their annual
discussions over their affairs. Not one person put in
an appearance at the place he had appointed, but they
all, as was their custom, faithfully attended their
religious services.

In solitary grandeur the representative of the Government was allowed to remain in his tent, with his
attendants, until the following day, and then the
Indians were promptly on hand to attend to business.

OLYMPIAN RANGE FROM ESQUIMAULT.

INDIAN MISSION WORK IN BRITISH COLUMBIA.*

It is no idle boast of the Methodist Church that it is pre-eminently a Missionary Church; and in this fact it has established its claim, beyond all controversy, as being in the true Apostolic succession. It is not too much to say that in no period of the Church's history have the triumphs of the Cross in heathen lands

* By J. E. McMillan, in *Methodist Magazine.*

been more signal or cheering to the friends of missionary enterprise than at this present moment, nor have there ever been so many open doors inviting the ambassadors of the Cross to enter and proclaim " the unsearchable riches of Christ."

Methodism was established in British Columbia late in the year 1858, or beginning of 1859, but little or nothing was done in the way of Christianizing the natives until about the year 1864, when Rev. T. Crosby entered upon the work as a lay teacher at Nanaimo. He readily acquired a knowledge of the native dialect of the people, and here the first converts from heathenism were won for Christ, of whom not a few have passed on to the " better land " in the triumphs of faith, while others remain until this day, witnessing a good profession and adorning the doctrines of Christ by a holy life and godly conversation. Subsequently, on the Frazer River, Mr. Crosby carried the message of a free salvation to the natives of that section, which they gladly received, and by faith in the simple story of the Cross were made happy partakers of the Saviour's love. The seed there sowed by Mr. Crosby fell upon good ground, and brought forth fruit an hundredfold, and the harvest of precious souls is still going on under the energetic and self-denying labours of Rev. C. M. Tate, Rev. A. E. Green and other devoted missionaries.

It was not until November, 1869, that an effort was put forth by a few friends of the cause of Jesus in Victoria, to do something to ameliorate the moral and religious condition of the natives resident in this

vicinity.   There was at this time a large Indian population in Victoria, representing tribes throughout
the whole country, from Frazer River to Queen
Charlotte's Island, a distance of about eight hundred
miles, and a more vicious and degraded class of people
could scarcely be found anywhere on earth.   Bad
apparently by nature, they were made infinitely worse
by contact with the whites, whose vices they readily
acquired, and became moral pests to the community.

At a meeting held in the house of Mr. Wm. McKay
in the month of November, 1869, it was resolved
to undertake the organization of

A SABBATH-SCHOOL AMONG THE INDIANS,

notwithstanding it was the opinion of some present
that the task was a hopeless one, the nat ves of the
place being so utterly depraved that not even the
Gospel could make any salutary impression upon
them.

Messrs. Wm. McKay and Alfred Lyne were deputed
as a kind of prospecting committee to visit the Songish
camp and ascertain what number, if any, could be
induced to join the school.   The old people listened
to what the committee had to say, were quite willing
to help the school along if paid for so doing, but
when informed that there was no "chickamin"
(money) in the enterprise, they declined to have
anything to do with it   Some of the younger people,
however, took a more favourable view of the matter,
among whom were Amos Sa-hat-ston and wife, who
gave in their names, and from the first took a lively

interest in the welfare of the school. At first not more than three or four could be persuaded to attend, but by careful management and much prayer for divine direction the number gradually increased to eight or ten.

On the 2nd of February, 1870, Amos Sa-hat-ston and two other Indians of the same tribe experienced the converting grace of God, and, after the usual three months' probation, were baptized and received

INDIANS FISHING THROUGH THE ICE.

into the Church. For upwards of six years Amos walked humbly before God, was ever present at class and prayer-meetings, and took a deep interest in the spiritual welfare of his people, until God, "who doeth all things well," called him from earth to heaven in the fall of 1876, after a few days' illness of small-pox. No sooner did Amos and his friends experience a change of heart than they began earnestly to exhort their brethren to seek the same blessing, and engaged audibly in prayer whenever an opportunity offered.

A REMARKABLE CONVERSION.

Until the fall of 1872 the number attending the school was seldom or never more than from ten to a dozen of the Songish tribe, and not unfrequently was it reduced to three or four. At this time, however, a circumstance occurred which led to one of the most remarkable revivals of religion ever recorded in the history of the natives of this or any country. One Sabbath morning, in the month of October, 1872, an Indian woman, named Elizabeth Diex, a chieftess of the Tshimpsean tribe, happening to pass by the school-house during the hour of service, and hearing singing going on inside, asked a little girl standing at the door what was doing there, and, on being told, inquired whether she would be at liberty to go in? Being answered in the affirmative, she opened the door and entered and took a seat. She watched the proceedings carefully, and retired at the close very much pleased with all she had seen and heard, and resolved to go again. Next Sabbath at the same hour she again visited the school, and on invitation of one of the teachers took a seat in one of the classes

She had received some precious instruction, could say her letters correctly, and even read a little in the First Book of Lessons; besides which she could converse tolerably well in English and understood pretty much all the teachers said. At this meeting one of the female teachers were called on and engaged in prayer, and, as she prayed with great earnestness and power, Elizabeth Diex, as she afterwards remarked,

could not resist the temptation to look around and
see what kind of a book she was praying from, and
to her great surprise discovered that the lady was
not using a book at all. This was the first time she
ever heard a person pray without a book, and was
greatly surprised that such a thing was possible. On

INDIAN TYPE.   SQUAW WITH HALF-BREED PAPOOSE.

the afternoon of the same day she attended school
again, and brought a friend or two with her. On
this occasion she heard Amos engage in prayer, using
the Chinook language, every word of which she
understood, and was deeply impressed with all she
had wisnessed and heard.

The next Sabbath, at the close of the school, she made a request that the "good white people" of the school would visit her house some evening during the week and hold a prayer-meeting for the benefit of herself and such of her Tshimpsean friends as she could in the meantime induce to attend. The following Wednesday evening was agreed upon, and at the appointed hour some half-dozen whites attended, found everything in readiness, and some eight or ten Indian friends present. That meeting proved to be the beginning of a revival which lasted continuously for nine weeks, and resulted in the conversion of upwards of forty natives. Among the first-fruits of this revival was Elizabeth Diex herself, a woman of commanding appearance and great force of character. Being an hereditary chieftess among her people, she exerts a great influence over them, and is a power for good among them. No sooner did she experience a change of heart, and realize the power of divine grace in the soul, than she entered into the work of bringing others to Christ with a zeal and devotion such as is but rarely equalled even among those who have had all the advantages of early Christian training.

At Fort Simpson, five hundred miles from Victoria, only fifteen miles from the Alaska frontier, she had an only son, whom she had not seen for years, who was noted as a desperate character, and held in dread by all who knew him. Almost the first thought of this Indian mother, after God spoke peace to her own soul, was for her wild and reckless son, and she "took him to the Lord in prayer," spending whole nights wrestling with God that her son might be induced to visit Victoria and be converted. This she told more than once in the meetings, and asked the prayers of God's people on behalf of her "wicked son, Alfred."

At this very time, and as she afterwards told us, after spending a whole night in earnest prayer to God, her son, Alfred, with his wife and child and some ten or a dozen other natives, arrived at Victoria in a large northern canoe direct from Fort Simpson. Some people would call this "a remarkable coincidence;" Professor Tyndall would ascribe it to "chance;" but believers in prayer will see in it a direct answer by God to the effectual, fervent prayer of a believing mother.

Scarcely had Alfred Dudoward and his wife, Kate, taken their seats under the maternal roof when the faithful mother opened up to them the subject of religion, and told them of the "pearl of great price" she herself had found. Alfred listened respectfully to what his mother had to say, but intimated that he had no desire to share in her religious enjoyment. That evening the mother attended the meeting alone, but the greater part of that night was spent by her in conversation with her children on the subject of religion and in prayer to God on their behalf. The next evening Alfred consented to go with his wife and mother to the meeting, and sat a silent spectator of what was passing before him. He retired with a stubborn will, but a convicted conscience. Not so his wife; she heard the words of eternal life, believed there was a reality in what she witnessed, and made

up her mind to seek and obtain the blessing her
mother and others had found. It was with great re-
luctance and after much persuasion by his mother
that Alfred was induced again to attend the meeting.
He did so, however, and the arrow of conviction found
a lodgment in his heart, and before the meeting closed
he was on his knees crying for mercy, and finally found
peace in believing, as did his wife also.

The conversion of this couple was the first fruits of
what has subsequently been developed into a rich
harvest of precious souls and the establishment of the

FORT SIMPSON MISSION.

Both Alfred and his wife Kate could speak English,
and also read and write. The latter, in her youthful
days, had received the benefit of a tolerably fair
English education under the instruction of the Sisters
of Charity in Victoria, which has proved to be a blessing to the Tshimpsean people, little dreamed of by
the good sisters when storing her mind with useful
knowledge. Both Alfred and Kate entered heartily
into the spirit of the revival, and were a great assistance alike to whites and natives during the progress
of the work. After the revival meetings had been
brought to a close, there were some six or eight of the
converted natives who could read a little in the Bible,
and at their request a Bible-class was established at
the house of Mrs. Diex. They would have made very
slow progress had it not been for Kate, who readily
translated into Tshimpsean what the teacher said ;
and frequently, as she would get interested in the

subject of the lesson, she would stand up with the Bible in her hand, and, looking at the text, read it off in Tshimpscan, while the tears of those who heard her would be seen trickling down the cheeks as she explained to them the story of Jesus and His love.

HALF-BREED INDIAN.   INDIAN LAD.

After a residence of nearly ten months in Victoria, Alfred and Kate Dudoward, with eight or ten others, left for their homes at Fort Simpson. They carried with them a dozen Bibles, several copies of the Methodist Catechism, and fifty copies of the First Book of Lessons, Canadian Series, the gift of kind friends in

Victoria. On arriving at their northern homes they immediately set to work to organize a school and hold religious services among their people. The change that had been wrought in the conduct and temper of Alfred, caused no little surprise to those who knew what his previous character had been. The desperado, who, but a few months before, was the terror of the whole surrounding country, had all at once become a meek and quiet citizen and a zealous-working Christian

"Old things had passed away, and behold, all things had become new." The chiefs and old men of the place wanted to know what all this meant, and what had so changed the character of the lion-hearted Alfred ? Alfred at once told the story of his conversion, of the wonderful work he had witnessed in Victoria, and of the resolution he and his wife and friends had come to, to endeavor, as best they could, to point the people of Fort Simpson to the " Lamb of God that taketh away the sin of the world," until a missionary could be obtained to take charge of the work. The same means employed at Victoria were adopted at Fort Simpson, namely, the reading and exposition of God's Word so far as they knew how, prayer and experience meetings, and the organization of classes. Besides this, Alfred and his wife commenced a dayschool, which in a very short time was attended by upwards of two hundred pupils.

Letter after letter was received by friends in Victoria urging them to use their influence to procure the appointment of a missionary for Fort Simpson, and for fully nine months did these people, pending the arrival of a missionary, carry on this remarkable work themselves, aided only by the operations of the Divine Spirit. When the Rev. W. Pollard, Chairman of the District, visited Fort Simpson, in the Spring of 1874, he wrote on his return as follows: " Not fewer than five hundred people attend the means of grace, some of whom are hopefully converted to God. There is not a family in Fort Simpson that has not renounced paganism, and is impatiently waiting the arrival of the missionary. When Mr. Crosby and his devoted and accomplished wife arrived at the scene of their future labors they found a glorious work going on, and were received by the people of their charge with such demonstrations of rejoicing as must have inspired them with a feeling of devout thankfulness to God for all he had done for those natives of the forest, and for having permitted them to be chosen as instruments in His hands to continue the work so auspiciously begun.

One of the first things Mr. Crosby did on his arrival at Fort Simpson was to call a meeting of his " parishioners," and ascertain from them what they were willing to contribute towards the erection of a church and parsonage. They told him they were willing to do all they could, and backed up their words by substantial contributions of money and money's worth to the extent of several hundred dollars, and soon they had a church capable of seating eight hundred persons—in fact, the most commodious Methodist church in the Province, and a comfortable parsonage

12

for the missionary. Its size was forty by fifty feet, with a spire one hundred and ten feet high. Much of the material for the church was contributed and much of the work was done by the Indians themselves.

SABBATH-KEEPING INDIANS.

The consistency and religious zeal of the converted Indians are as remarkable as praiseworthy. It is customary in the spring of the year for a number of the Fort Simpson Indians to go to the mines at Cassiar, finding employment on the way as packers. During the spring of 1876 several Tshimpsean Indians engaged to pack a quantity of goods for a company of miners, and worked faithfully day after day until Saturday evening came, when tents were pitched. Sunday morning the miners prepared to proceed on their journey, but were quietly informed by their native packers that they could not do so, it being the Sabbath day, on which they would do no work. The miners stormed and swore, and threatened what they would do if the Indians did not proceed, but all to no purpose ; they would not move, so the miners had to yield to circumstances they could not control, and keep the Sabbath day. The reading of the Bible and singing hymns occupied the time during the day, and on Monday morning they proceeded on their journey, all the better for having enjoyed a day of rest.

Fort Wrangel is the chief stopping-place for miners and traders going to and returning from the Cassiar mines. Besides a military and an Indian camp, there are a larger number of miners and traders who make

that their place of rendezvous and residence. A more ungodly place could scarcely be found on the face of the earth. The population was almost wholly given over to drunkenness, gambling, and debauchery of the worst kind, and there were none to reprove their wickedness until the spring of 1876, when several Fort Simpson Indians arrived there *en route* for the mines. As the river was not free of ice, the town was full of people awaiting the opening of navigation, our Indian friends among the rest. In the face of the most adverse circumstances—mocked and jeered at by many of the "superior" white race—those faithful witnesses for Christ obtained a place that had been used as a dance-house, in which to hold religious services, and at once set to work to gather in as many of the natives of the place as they could to hear the word of life. At first the attendance was small, but the number gradually increased till the place was quite inadequate to hold all who sought admission. God owned the labours of those faithful men, and quite a number of the natives of Wrangel were brought from the darkness of heathenism to the light of the Gospel, among the rest the head chief of the place.

For weeks and months the voice of praise and prayer were heard daily at Wrangel, the services being conducted wholly by native agency. As the place is under military rule, the commanding officer became much interested in the work, and enforced good order at the meeting. A custom prevailed amongst the Indians there, when one of their number

died, of placing the body upon a pile, in the centre
of one of their large lodges, setting fire to it, and then
dancing and howling around the burning corpse until
it was totally consumed. To this horrid practice the
Fort Simpson Indians were instrumental in putting
an end. They obtained a grant of a piece of land
from the commandant of the place for a burial-ground,
and buried the first Indian who died thereafter with
all the rites peculiar to civilized life. There is now
at Wrangel, as the result of the labours of those
faithful natives, a mission, established under the
auspices of the American Presbyterian Church, that
place being beyond the ecclesiastical jurisdiction of
our Church.

NAAS RIVER MISSION.

As at Fort Wrangel, so at Naas River—the first to
carry the message of salvation to that people were
the converted natives of Fort Simpson, if we except
what little light some of them may have obtained at
Mr. Tomlinson's station, near the mouth of the river,
which is conducted partly as a trading post and partly
as a mission station. As to the extent of spiritual
profit derived from this mission, let the Indians
themselves bear testimony, as they do in the sub-
joined address to Rev. Messrs. Green and Crosby. In
the face of repeated threats of personal violence did
William Henry Laknate and George Pemberton, both
natives of Fort Simpson, visit Naas River and preach
Jesus and Him crucified to the people there who sat
in heathen darkness. Mr. Crosby shortly followed

and repeated the "old, old story," and invited them to come to "the fountain of living waters," and also to " taste and see that the Lord is good."   At length the strong hearts began to soften and to yield to the influences of the Gospel.   Some of the Naas chiefs visited Fort Simpson and also Victoria, attended services in both places, after which they returned to their own homes, convinced that this religion which had been so freely offered to them was well worth accepting. All at once the desire to have a missionary became general, and a delegation was despatched to Fort Simpson to confer with Mr. Crosby as to how they might obtain one.   Mr. Crosby promised that he would do all he could for them—would write to the missionary authorities at Toronto and lay their case before them, and in the meantime he would visit them himself as frequently as possible.

At the district meeting held in Victoria in 1876, Mr. Crosby, in reporting upon the work in his circuit, brought up the question of a missionary for Naas River.   He told how these people had visited him ; how urgently they desired a missionary ; what a vast field was there to be taken up, and not fewer than fifteen hundred precious souls calling for the Gospel. Something, he said, must be done in answer to this call for the Word of Life from these perishing heathen, and he begged of his ministerial brethren to join with him in asking the Missionary Committee to appoint a man to Naas River.   Every man in that meeting, clerical and lay, heartily sympathized with Mr. Crosby, as, with tears in his eyes, he pleaded the cause of the

people of Nass River, but they felt that it would be
useless to ask the Missionary Committee to take up

ON THE LOWER FRASER.

new ground in view of the greatly depressed condition of the Missionary Society's finances, and the
chairman of the district, for the reasons stated, said

he could not recommend an appropriation for that purpose. " Well," said Mr. Crosby, " this call is of God, and *must* be attended to." Mr. Green, whose time would shortly be up at Wellington, said, if appointed to Naas he would go if he should not be guaranteed a dollar for his support, believing that the God of missions would provide for all his temporal necessities. This occurred on a Saturday afternoon, and when the meeting adjourned Mr. Crosby, as he afterwards remarked, retired to his closet and spent an hour in earnest prayer to God that the way might be opened up for Mr. Green or someone else to go to Naas.

That same evening a prayer meeting was held at the house of Mr. McKay, in the same room where the first meeting was held in 1869 to consider what could be done for the spiritual welfare of the natives in Victoria, and at the meeting Mr. Crosby was present, and asked for the prayers and sympathy of his brethren in behalf of the people of Naas River. He obtained both, and the meeting at once took a very decided missionary character. No one anticipated an appeal for funds on the occasion, nor did anyone ask for any. One kind brother, however, remarked that no doubt a fund of fifty dollars might be raised at once, in that room, toward helping forward the cause at Naas River, and that he himself would give ten dollars toward it. Soon $236 were pledged to aid the cause at Naas. Besides this, $137.50 were subsequently given for the same cause, not a dollar of which was solicited from any individual.

After reaching Naas River the chiefs gave Mr. Green and Mr. Crosby a hearty welcome. One old chief, as he leaned upon his staff, said : " I am getting old; my body is getting weaker every day; I am obliged to have three legs to walk with now (referring to his staff); this tells me I shall soon die ; I don't know what hour I shall be called away ; I want to hear about the great God, and I want my children to be taught to read the good Book ; I want them to go in the new way ; I am tired of the old fashion." Another said, as he pointed up the river : " There are ten tribes of people living up there. Missionary, we give them all to you ! Go and see them ; they all want to hear about the Great Spirit." Mr. Green then goes on to say : " Brother Crosby stayed with me five days. We held three services each day, and all the people attended ; and the best of all was God was with us, blessing His word, so that this great heathen house was filled with the cries of penitents seeking for salvation, who now stand up in class-meeting and say they are happy in Jesus ; so that we have a class of twenty members who profess to have passed from death to life by simple faith in Jesus. We look upon these as the first fruits of what we have abundant cause to hope will be a great and glorious harvest."

In a subsequent letter, Mr. Green writes: " The Lord is greatly blessing His Word, so that we have had a glorious outpouring of the Holy Spirit all the time since the first week of our arrival here. The interest does not diminish, but increases every day. Men come daily to ask how they can settle their old heathen dance debts, as they want to love God and be Christians. One old doctor came with tears in his eyes to tell me he was so sorry he talked bad about me and opposed our work. He had not eaten any food nor slept for three days, as his heart was so troubled ; and now he wanted me to forgive him and pray with him. We knelt down and prayed together, and God answered our prayer by setting his soul at liberty." "My congregations," he further adds, "average about five hundred. They all come to prayer-meeting, and one hundred meet in class."

Never was a people more anxious to receive the light of the Gospel, and thousands along the whole coast of this Province are, like the Macedonians of old, calling aloud for the missionaries of the Cross to "come over and help them." "The harvest truly is great, but the labourers are few." The following is a copy of an address presented to Mr. Green and Mr. Crosby on the occasion of their first visit to Naas River :

"We, the chiefs and people of the Naas, welcome you from our hearts on your safe arrival here, to begin in earnest the mission work you promised us last spring when you visited us. We have seen the mission carried on about fifteen miles from us, at the mouth of the river, for many years, but cannot see much good it has done to our poor people ; but as you say you do not come to trade with us, but only to teach us, we think it will be very different under your instruction, and we tell you that we will do what we can to assist you in the good work.

SALMON WHEEL AND FISHERMEN.

This wheel, revolving with the force of the current, catches the fish as they swim up the river, and throws them into the barge.

"Our past life has been bad—*very bad.* We have been so long left in darkness that we fear you will not be able to do much for our old people ; but for our young we have great hopes. We wish from our hearts to have our young men, women and children read and write, so that they may understand the duties they owe to their great Creator and to each other.

"You will find great difficulties in the way of such work, but great changes cannot be expected in one day. You must not get discouraged by a little trouble, and we tell you again that we will all help you as much as we can.

"We believe this work to be of God. We have prayed as you told us, and now we think that God has heard our prayers and sent you to us, and it seems to us like the day breaking in on our darkness, and we think that before long the Great Sun will shine upon us and give us more light.

"We hope to see the white men that settle among us set us a good example ; as they have had the light so long, they know what is right and what is wrong. We hope they will assist us to do what is good, that we may become better and better every day by following their example.

"We again welcome you from our hearts, and hope that the mission here will be like a great rock, never to be moved or washed away ; and in order to this we will pray to the Great Spirit that His blessing may rest upon this mission and upon us all.

(Signed)   "CHIEF OF THE MOUNTAINS.

"*And six other Chiefs.*"

Rev. Thomas Crosby.

Nearly thirty years of toil and travel and self-denying effort for the evangelization of the Indians of the great North-West, have made the names of Thomas Crosby and wife household words throughout Canada. Few people, even among those who knew them best, have any idea of the extent of their labours. The change visible in some localities is witnessed—groups of Indians quit their vicious lives, the women and girls become virtuous and decent; a church is built, and the whole settlement is revolutionized. Then the man and his wife, whose labours have been blessed of God to this glorious result, cease to be residents of the district. They disappear, but they are gratefully remembered, and their frequent visits afterward are festivals to be anticipated, enjoyed and recollected with delight. Where do they go? The people whom they have served so well do not always know; but, if inquiry is made, they learn that the work that has been done among them is being done with the same laborious effort and the same joyful results in some other settlement. No less than thirteen hundred persons have in this way been brought into Church membership, and have joyfully professed their faith in Christ. More than six thousand have heard the Gospel and been brought under Christian influences in church and Sunday-school. This, in a thinly settled country, where means of communication are few and precarious, is a stupendous work for one man to have accomplished, involving almost inconceivable labour and hardship.

The instrument God has used for the achievement of this enormous undertaking seemed, to human eyes, a very unsuitable one. With little education, no college training and no preparatory study, he took up

REV. THOMAS CROSBY.

the work, moved by faith and love; and by simple brotherly affection and quiet, unobtrusive helpfulness he won the good-will of the people in one section after another and led them to Christ. The word of call and inspiration was as simple as it was effectual.

In the year 1860 there appeared in a Canadian journal a letter signed " Edward White," in which the writer dwelt on the urgent need of the country. " Thousands of young men," he said, "are coming to British Columbia seeking gold; but where are the young men whom we need to consecrate their youth and strength to the preaching of the Gospel to the miners and the Indians?"

It was a deplorable picture that he drew of the condition of these people. They were leading lives of practical heathenism ; the miners careless, dissolute and depraved, and the Indians sacrificing the sacred ties of fatherhood and brotherhood in pandering to the vices of the white settlers, and squandering the poor proceeds in self-indulgence. It was an awful circle of mutual corruption, vice and degradation. Who was there with faith in God and conviction in his soul of the purifying and elevating power of the Gospel, who would go and preach it and live it among them ? It was like asking for volunteers for a forlorn hope, or for missionaries for some benighted island of the South Seas, with the added difficulty that some of those to whom it was proposed to send the Gospel were backsliders from Christian lands.

We do not know how many read that appeal from Edward White, but we know that one young man read it, and could not forget it.

Thomas Crosby was then twenty years old. Four years before he had come from an English village to Woodstock with his father, mother and brothers, and had settled here. The family was poor, and the father's venture in farming, which at first promised a brilliant success, ended disastrously. The boy must earn his own living, and he took the first opportunity. He went to work in a tannery, and was making his way. In his seventeenth year he became a member of the Methodist church in Woodstock, and after a short time was appointed a local preacher. To him Edward White's letter appeared to be a personal call. He dwelt upon it, re-read it, took it to his room and read it on his knees, and finally made an offer of himself in solemn consecration to God for the work. That was all he could do; he left the opening of the way to God. Two days later he had an intimation that his offer was accepted. His elder brother, an unconverted man, spontaneously removed the only difficulty in the way by offering him all the money he needed. " Take it as a loan, Tom," he said; "if you can repay it, do; if not, I shall never ask you for it." He took the money, and going to his room, he knelt down and thanked God for it, and said that henceforth his whole life was given up to Him.

The matter was settled there and then. All attempts to dissuade him from an enterprise that seemed to the worldly mind profitless and foolhardy, failed. His employer was the first to assail him. " What are these people to you ?" he asked. " They are savages; they will kill you and eat you. Don't be quixotic; stay with us; you have done well, and may do better. Keep on with your work, and from to-day we will double your wages." Tom had but one answer for the kindly tanner: He had promised God and must

go. At home the trial was harder. The father could
not see the call in the light that Tom saw it; his
mother wept over her boy, and declared that she could
not spare him. There was a midnight scene that is
still fresh in his memory, when father and mother
both listened to his story of the call and the consecration, and lamented over him as one given over to
death. " I cannot be happy if I don't go," Tom said.
Then his mother answered, with a voice broken by
sobs: " Well, then, my boy, go, and God bless you."
Hundreds of times in after years, on storm-tossed seas
and lonely desert places, in the solemn night hours,
Mr. Crosby declares, the echo of those words fell on
his ears, encouraging him and stimulating him. The
ejaculatory prayer was heard and abundantly answered.
God has blessed him.

Setting out alone on his perilous enterprise, with
no promise of support from any Church or society, he
made his way to Victoria, British Columbia, where he
arrived April 11th, 1862. He was anxious to enter on
his work unhampered by an obligation, so he stayed
there working with his hands until he had earned
enough money to repay his brother's loan. The time
was not lost; he gained much knowledge of the field,
and he gained strength in lonely communion with
God. It was the period of solitude which generally
precedes a life of consecrated work. Moses and John
the Baptist, and even the Master himself, prepared
for their labours in retirement from the world.

About a year after his arrival at Victoria, he went
to Dr. Evans and told him of his purpose. As a

13

practical preparation, Dr. Evans sent him to Nanaimo, Vancouver Island, to teach the first

INDIAN MISSION SCHOOL

that had been established.   There he laboured and taught and learned.   In six months he was able to

MRS. THOMAS CROSBY.

understand the Indian Flathead language, and before the first year was out he could preach in that tongue. Life began in earnest with that acquisition, and Crosby lost no opportunity of exercising it.   He journey in all directions from his school; preaching the Gospel in the Indian huts and tents and in the open air, and living with the Indians as one of themselves. Soon it was necessary to build a church at Chilliwack. There, to his great delight, he received a visit from Dr. Punshon, who preached in the new church. Learning that he had not been ordained, Dr. Punshon surprised him by proposing to confer ordination upon him. Crosby had scruples on account of his lack of a college education, of his lack of theological training and general unfitness; but Dr. Punshon overcame them, declaring that Crosby had given the best of all proofs of his fitness in his success.

Mr. Crosby remained in that field two years longer, and then returned to Victoria to report his success to the church there, in the hope of getting some thoroughly organized work for reaching the Indians commenced. Two of the brethren there, McKay and McMillan, were deeply interested in his story, and made the experiment of mission services in Victoria itself. They hired a bar-room on the corner of Government and Fitzgerald Streets, and Crosby gladly preached in it. There were plenty of Indians there who had come down from the north with their squaws and daughters to engage in their loathsome traffic. A great work began in that bar-room. and many of the people converted during those services, more than twenty years ago, are still living, and are leading earnest, faithful Christian lives. Their rescue from the horrible life they were living, and from the degrading purpose for which they went to Victoria, was a marvel to them, and they begged the man who had been instrumental in effecting it to return with them to Fort Simpson, that their relatives and neighbours might hear the good tidings, too. He was unable to comply, but promised to visit them soon.

During the next few months Mr. Crosby went to Ontario, arousing the churches to the need of the work, and awakening them by his story of what had already been accomplished, and by his testimony as to the readiness of the Indian to listen to the Gospel, to the duty of supporting missionaries among them. During that tour he incidentally awakened in one of his hearers another kind of interest, which finally became a very close and personal one. He was married to the daughter of Rev. John Douse, and henceforth had a valuable helper in his work.

On the conclusion of his tour, Mr. Crosby kept his promise to the Indians whom he had served at Victoria. A Hudson's Bay ship, sailing to Alaska, carried the missionary and his wife to Fort Simpson, about seventy miles from Mr. Duncan's station at Metlakahtla. The converts of the Victoria work had prepared the way for his coming, and Mr. Crosby was received with open arms. After a short time a church was organized and a building commenced. Mr. Crosby, with his own hands, cut the timber, and the Indians laboured hard at the building. The skilled labour was paid for chiefly by the Indians themselves, who, although they had no money, brought furs, finger-rings, ear-rings and surplus blankets, and gave them freely for the building fund. The completion of the church was the beginning of a wonderful work of grace, which spread to distant places. The people who came to Fort Simpson and heard the Gospel went home, and soon messages came from them to Mr. Crosby, begging him to visit them. He went to Queen Charlotte Sound, where there was a similar ingathering of souls ; thence to Bella Bella, to Bella Coola and to many other places. In each settlement he remained preaching and teaching until a church was organized, and he could safely proceed to a new field.

THE "GLAD TIDINGS."

The extremities of this chain of missionary stations were two hundred miles apart, and this distance was covered by Mr. Crosby, in his journeyings to and fro, by canoe. For more than ten years he kept up this laborious and often perilous mode of travel, rowing, on an average, 2,000 miles in a year. But in 1882 he realized that some better mode of locomotion could no longer be dispensed with. He must have a steamboat, which would save time and labour. Remembering his former success in Ontario, he returned there, and, lecturing and appealing to the churches, he succeeded in raising a small fund for the purpose. With the aid of a sailor, who had been converted in one of his meetings, he built the boat; a small engine, which would propel it at the rate of seven knots an hour, was purchased and put in, and thus equipped, Mr. Crosby resumed his labours.

The statistical results of these long years of labour are remarkable. There are now twenty-three churches in regular organization, with day-schools and Sunday-schools; an hospital, under the charge of a skilful Christian physician; a large industrial school for girls, with forty pupils, and a similar institution for boys, where instruction is given in useful arts. There are eight ordained ministers, seven lay missionaries

MISSION STEAM YACHT "GLAD TIDINGS."

and eight native assistants. The churches are self-supporting, and are in a most thriving condition. Looking back on the results of his thirty years of labour, Mr. Crosby thanks God that he was led to take up this pioneer work, and for the success with which God has rewarded him.